Fiona Beckett   Will Beckett

an Appetite
for ALE

photography by Vanessa Courtier

Published by the Campaign for Real Ale, 230 Hatfield Road,
St Albans, Hertfordshire AL1 4LW

www.camra.org.uk/books

Text © 2007 Fiona Beckett and Will Beckett
Design and layout © 2007 Campaign for Real Ale Ltd
Photography © 2007 Vanessa Courtier

ISBN: 978-1-85249-234-2
A CIP catalogue record for this book is available from the British Library
Printed in Singapore by KHL Printing Co Pte Ltd

Head of Publications: Joanna Copestick
Managing Editor: Simon Hall
Editor: Helen Ridge
Editorial Assistance: Debbie Williams, Emma Lloyd
Photography: Vanessa Courtier
Design and Art Direction: Vanessa Courtier
Production: redbus
Marketing Manager: Georgina Rudman

Contents

Introduction 7

Soups, spreads & snacks 12

Pasta, antipasti & risotto 36

Seafood 48

Chicken & other birds 66

Meat feasts 82

Spicy food 104

Salads & veg 120

Bread & cheese 134

Sweet treats 144

Entertaining with beer 164

Conversion charts 184

Index 185

'What two ideas are more inseparable than Beer and Britannia?'

Sydney Smith (1771–1845)

From pint to pot

From the amount of space devoted to the subject in the media you'd think that wine, rather than beer, was our national drink. Yet beer drinking has been woven into the fabric of life in this country for not only centuries but millennia. Unlike wine, which was the drink of the privileged few, beer, or more accurately ale – a strong, sweet, unhopped brew – was the drink of the working poor; far safer than water and far more nourishing than much of the food that would have been available. It was, indeed, liquid bread.

Maybe it never overcame that association. Beer has never been elevated to the status it enjoys in Belgium or in Germany, where the rigorous purity laws have accorded it an iconic status. Walking through the streets of London's Soho, you'll see pavements crowded with office workers (mainly male), pint glass in hand, yet those same workers wouldn't dream of ordering a beer with their dinner afterwards or putting it on the table at home (except with a takeaway curry).

In the course of researching this book, we've travelled to other beer-producing countries, where beer is far more closely woven into the fabric of social life: to Belgium, where fine-dining restaurants, such as Bruges's Den Djver, are the norm; to Munich, where the world's most famous beer festival attracts old and young alike, as intent on eating as drinking; and to the US, where the fantastic resurgence in craft beers has got even huge players like Anheuser-Busch keen to show how well their beers pair with food.

It's something we've tried to push, too. At his award-winning North London gastropub The Marquess Tavern, Will and his business partner Huw Gott have set out to show that 'gastropub' doesn't simply mean a place with a smart wine list, but a genuine choice of interesting beers, picked for their compatibility with food. Meanwhile, as a food and drink writer, I've written and enthused about the virtues of beer and food whenever I've managed to twist the arm of an editor willing to concede that his or her readers might be as interested in a pint of real ale as a glass of chardonnay.

We hope this book will do its bit to change perceptions of beer and its place on the dinner table. We're not ashamed to admit that we've learnt a great deal from writing it – and that we've only begun to scratch the surface of the subject. We hope that you'll enjoy your beer even more as a result of reading the book and sharing the recipes with your friends.

Fiona Beckett   Will Beckett

Matching beer & food

Matching beer and food has a bit of a prescriptive ring about it, we admit, as if there are right and wrong answers. Of course, you should drink the beer that you like with the food you enjoy but it's possible to get stuck in a rut and miss out on some flavour combinations that are quite simply stunning.

As you've probably already discovered, beer behaves differently from wine when it comes to food. Most beer lacks acidity and tannin, two qualities that help wine match well. But it has other qualities, such as bitterness, sweetness, carbonation, lower levels of alcohol and, most importantly, a range of flavours you simply don't find in wine (chocolate, smoke and caramel, to name just three), that more than compensate.

The most significant of these qualities is bitterness, which is not likely to bother you if you're a beer lover to start with but it may bother friends that you're trying to get to share your enthusiasm. Where food is concerned, the bitterness of beer is a double-edged sword. It can be intrusive and jarring, much as an over-exuberant use of oak can be in wine, but it's also incredibly refreshing, especially with foods that are sour, salty, fatty or in other ways palate-coating, like chocolate and cheese.

There are two types of bitterness: hop bitterness and roasted malt bitterness. Hop bitterness works fantastically well with spices, which is why IPAs are such a great match for spicy food, while roasted malt bitterness has a palate-cleansing quality, which can help with such disparate foods as roast or barbecued meats, cheese and chocolate. With a rich chocolate dessert, for example, you don't want yet more richness in your glass. You want something that is going to be refreshing, like a bitter porter or a sour wheat beer.

Complement or contrast?

People often talk about complementing or contrasting flavours with beer, but we think that's an unnecessarily complicated approach. All you need to ask yourself is 'What sort of a drink do I want with this dish or this meal?'. And that's a question of balance. If you know the flavours are going to be delicate, as they would be in a salad or a seafood risotto, you want a beer that won't overwhelm them, such as a Pilsener or a wheat beer. If the flavours are full, as they would be in a steak and ale pie or a beef stew, you want a beer of equal weight, like a traditional British or Belgian Trappist ale. If the flavours are extreme – very hot, spicy or sweet – you want a beer that offers some respite and refreshment.

A similar common sense approach applies to deciding the order in which to serve beers. In general, it's better to drink lighter, drier beers before richer, sweeter, more powerful ones, just as you serve lighter dishes before more intensely flavoured foods.

Light or dark?

The terms can be confusing. If you're just getting into beer, you may not have fully grasped that beers don't always taste as they look. A light colour doesn't necessarily mean a light beer, as those of you who have tried strong Belgian golden ales like Duvel will know. Nor does the fact that a beer is dark mean that it's powerful – think of traditional British brown ales, like Manns, or stouts, like Mackeson. So, let flavour, rather than colour, be your guide.

Carbonation – or the lack of it

The other factor to take into account when matching beer and food is carbonation. Of course, this is more pronounced in some beers, such as wheat beers or Pilseners, than in others, like traditional British ales, and virtually non-existent in a few, such as strong barley wines. But, again, if your palate is likely to be under assault from deep-fried, spicy or fatty foods, look to a beer where carbonation is more pronounced.

Carbonated drinks also support flavours better than still ones. If you drink a peach-flavoured dessert wine with a peach-flavoured dessert, for example, the dessert will strip the peach flavours from the wine. The carbonation of a peach-flavoured lambic beer, on the other hand, will preserve the fruit flavours of the beer, cleansing the palate between each mouthful and echoing but not overwhelming the flavours of the dessert. It means you can rely on flavour, rather than strength, or sweetness for a match, which, again, makes for a refreshing experience.

You'll find many more tips and specific pairings right the way through the book: in the introductions to each chapter, following each recipe, and in the food and beer matching charts at the end of the book, but don't let that stop you exploring other options. Individual beers vary hugely, even within a similar style (just think of IPAs), so keep on experimenting. The best way to learn about beer and food is at the table!

Comparing beer with wine

If you're more accustomed to drinking wine than beer, it may help to find the nearest style of beer to the wines that you're familiar with. Of course, some beers, including classic British bitters, stouts, porters and gueuze, simply don't have a wine equivalent. But that's part of their charm.

* Dry white wines **Light lagers; Pilseners**

* Medium- to full-bodied white wines, like chardonnay **Golden ales or lagers; blonde ales**

* Aromatic wines, like sauvignon blanc and riesling **Witbiers**

* Light reds, like pinot noir **Cherry and raspberry beers; sour red beers**

* Medium-bodied reds **Amber ales**

* Full-bodied reds **Full-bodied British ales; strong Belgian and northern French beers; abbey beers**

* Dessert wines **Fruit beers**

* Port **Porters; barley wines; doppelbocks**

* Champagne and sparkling wine **Beers fermented with champagne yeasts; Pilseners**

Beer-friendly flavours & ingredients

There are certain ingredients, dishes and cooking techniques that suit beer at least as well as, if not better than, wine. And we speak as wine lovers, too!

Shellfish From the classic combination of oysters and Guinness to witbier with crab or moules frîtes, beer and shellfish is a great combination. It's principally the saltiness that does it, though other tastes, like iodine and sweetness, come into play.

Smoked & cured foods Bacon, smoked sausages and smoked fish work well with all kinds of beer, from light lagers and Pilseners to smoked beers. There's a slight bitterness about smoke that picks up on both hops and malt.

Salty, brined & pickled foods Largely no-go areas for wine or, at least, a very tough pairing. Light lagers and Pilseners are the best match by far for foods like pickled herrings and pickled red cabbage, while IPAs can handle tricky-to-match chutneys, such as piccalilli.

Caramelized foods Roast and grilled meats, roast root vegetables and caramelized onions are all great partners for a hearty ale or an amber ale or lager.

Meaty sauces & stews, especially if cooked with beer Gastropub favourites, such as shepherd's pie and sausage and mash, are excellent with a traditional British ale, as are any dishes with gravy (as opposed to a concentrated red wine-based 'jus', which is obviously better with wine). Beer is also good with 'meaty' vegetarian ingredients, such as miso and mushrooms.

Anything savoury made with flour Bread, pies, pancakes, the proverbial beer and sandwiches, a good pork pie, a pasty…

Anything fried, battered or breadcrumbed Like fish and chips or southern fried chicken.

Barbecued foods The combination of sweetness, spiciness and smokiness tends to make for flavour overload, which makes beer a more refreshing accompaniment than wine.

Spicy food This includes not just curries but also spicy nibbles and noodles, for which there are many more interesting options than lager – IPA being the obvious example.

Dishes that include, or are accompanied by, mustard Mustard has a heat and bitterness that works really well with hops. Add it to a food that's already beer-friendly, such as sausages, and you're in beer heaven.

Cheese Apart from goats' cheese, we're not sure that most cheeses don't fare better with beer, especially strong, stinky French cheeses.

Chocolate A surprise, maybe, but if you haven't tried a chocolate mousse or roulade, such as the one on page 156, with a cherry or raspberry beer, you haven't lived. Dark smoky porter is also a good match for chocolate – just like an espresso coffee.

Foods that don't go so well with beer We know beer fans are reluctant to admit that anything doesn't go well with their favourite drink, but we would respectfully suggest that tomato-based Italian dishes and dishes in which lemon is the dominant note are generally better with wine. Not that you can't adjust the match, we hasten to add, by introducing more beer-friendly ingredients, such as pancetta, olives and hot peppers in the case of tomato-based dishes, or raw onions and strongly flavoured herbs like coriander in the case of lemon-flavoured ones.

Cooking with beer

Cooking with beer is very different from cooking with wine, and I confess I made a couple of howlers when I started out. One was deglazing a pan with beer, which left me nothing but the bitter taste of hops. The other was leaving some lamb shanks overnight in a Trappist ale and finding the next day that they'd gone off, so vigorous was the enzymatic activity!

I also discovered that using beer as the sole base for a stew or a sauce, as you can perfectly well do with wine, was likely to result in too bitter a flavour (you can, however, make jellies and sorbets with undiluted beer, which you can't do with undiluted wine).

For those of you who are new to cooking with beer, here are a few guidelines that may help.

＊ If you're using beer in a sauce or gravy, don't make it more than one-third to half the total liquid – this will obviously depend on the bitterness of the beer. The hoppier the brew, the less you need. If meat is included, as in the Cottage pie with porter on page 96 or the Carbonnade of beef with Orval on page 91, you can use slightly more.

＊ As beer generally lacks the acidity of wine and has more bitterness, you are likely to need to adjust the seasoning more carefully. To 'lift' a stew or casserole, I got into the habit of adding a little malt or cider vinegar. To counteract bitterness, I add a little malt extract, brown sugar or tomato ketchup. The important point is always to taste a dish before you serve up – a standard cooking tip but one that's even more critical where beer is involved.

＊ When you're deglazing a pan, add some stock or water first to bring the temperature down, then add the beer to avoid bitterness. If you want to glaze a dish, start with some oil or butter, and keep the temperature low.

＊ Remember that beer foams up when you pour it into a pan, so make sure that the pan is large enough for it not to overflow.

＊ Don't marinate longer than a couple of hours – you'll get the benefit of the beer flavour in that time.

＊ Do add beer to home-made batters and fritters – you'll get a much lighter, airier and crisper result.

＊ Bread also rises better if you add beer.

＊ Do add a splash of ale when you next make a cheese sauce – it really transforms the flavour. Experiment with different beers and different cheeses.

＊ Don't hesitate to add ingredients to a recipe to make it more beer-friendly, as I've done with the Smoky bacon bolognese on page 43 and Smoked fish pie on page 60. Pickled ingredients, such as capers and olives, also help to enhance a beer match.

" Do use freshly drawn or opened beer for cooking. Unlike wine, beer doesn't keep long once it's opened, which means you'll just have to drink up what you don't use. What a shame... "

soups, spreads & snacks

For many people, food with beer begins and ends with snacks. A few nuts and crisps. A sandwich or a ploughman's. A pie and a pint. A slice – or three – of pizza.

There's nothing wrong with that but there's no harm in taking it to a higher level. The nuts could be spiced – just minutes in the pan, the crisps bought in but handbaked, the sandwiches freshly made and crammed with filling, the pie from a farmers' market or local butcher instead of – no, we're sure you wouldn't do this – a garage forecourt. There's no reason why fast food needs to be junk food.

What most snacks have in common, of course, is carbs – and carbs and beer, especially traditional ales, are great bedfellows. In fact, bread is so near beer in character that they're simply two facets of the same product – one solid, one liquid, like non-identical twins.

This chapter also contains some good things to put on bread – some easy dips, spreads and pâtés that you could equally well use as a simple starter. There's a home-made (and healthy) version of a doner kebab, and cunning tips for dressing up shop-bought pizzas. There's a giant cheese, potato and onion pie, an easy-to-make alternative to a cheese and onion pasty, or you can head to the bread and cheese chapter for the perfect ploughman's on page 138. And if you're looking for spicy snacks, you'll find them on pages 106–7.

Finally, well, actually, first of all, there's soup, the healthiest snack of all. You might think that soup would be tricky to pair with beer and you'd be right. One liquid with another can feel strange but, because of its levels of carbonation, beer is a better accompaniment than wine. The kinds of soup that work best are robust, chunky soups, especially those based on beans and lentils, root vegetables like onions, beetroot, parsnips and potatoes, and bitter greens like cabbage. And, of course, beer and cheese soup is a classic.

Carrot borscht

A brilliant recipe from my daughter Jo, inspired by her organic veg box. It's a great way to use up some good, rich dark stock or, if you want to keep it veggie, use vegetable stock and leave out the bacon.

serves 4

3 tbsp organic sunflower or organic rapeseed oil

4 rashers of smoked streaky bacon, finely
  chopped

1 medium onion, peeled and finely chopped

2 medium carrots (about 175–200g),
  well scrubbed or peeled and grated

3 medium beetroot (about 300–350g), well
  scrubbed and peeled

1 tomato, skinned and roughly chopped
  (optional)

1 tsp chopped fresh thyme leaves
  or ½ tsp dried thyme

750ml ham, duck or beef stock or 750ml vegetable
  stock made with 1 level tbsp vegetable bouillon powder

a handful of beet greens, washed and shredded

sea salt, freshly ground black pepper and sugar or cider
  or wine vinegar, to taste

Heat 2 tbsp of the oil in a large saucepan or casserole and fry the bacon for a few minutes until the fat begins to run. Stir in the onion, turn the heat down, cover and cook for 4–5 minutes, then add the remaining oil and the grated carrot and continue to cook, covered, over a low heat.

Halve the beetroot, slice thinly, then slice across into short batons. Tip the beetroot and tomato, if using, into the bacon and other vegetables, stir, add the thyme and continue to cook for another 5 minutes. Add the stock and bring to the boil, then cook until the vegetables have softened (about 20 minutes). Season to taste with salt and pepper. Add a little sugar if you feel it needs it, or a few drops of vinegar if it needs sharpening up. Add the shredded greens, cook for a couple more minutes and serve. Good with rye bread or sourdough bread spread with a soft cheese like quark or goats' cheese.

Best beer match A Pilsener is perfect with this soup but we reckon it would also be pretty good with a stout, porter or dark lager.

Roast parsnip & onion soup

One of those serendipitous recipes that came about when there wasn't much in the veg rack but there were some parsnips to use up. Now it's one of my favourite soups. If you can't find the particular Earth's Energy spice grinder I use (see below), grind up some coriander, cumin, sesame and fennel seeds with some rough sea salt and black peppercorns.

serves 4
500g parsnips
1 large or 2 smaller onions
3 tbsp sunflower oil
Earth's Energy spice grinder (or a roughly ground
  mixture of cumin, coriander, fennel and sesame
  seeds – see above) *
800ml stock made with 1 tbsp vegetable bouillon
  powder
1 tsp ground coriander (optional)
2 tbsp finely chopped fresh coriander

Heat the oven to 180°C/350°F/Gas 4. Scrub the parsnips clean and cut into even-sized pieces, cutting away the central woody core.

Peel the onion and cut into rough chunks. Put the vegetables into a roasting tin, pour over the oil and add a good few grinds of the spice grinder (or a heaped teaspoon of freshly ground spices) and mix together well.

Roast for about 40–45 minutes until the vegetables are soft and well browned, turning them over halfway through and adding 1/2 a glass of water to stop them from drying out. Remove from the oven and cool a little.

Whizz the vegetables and any remaining liquid in the tin in a food processor (you may need to do this in two batches), gradually adding the stock to make a smooth purée.

Tip into a saucepan, add the remaining stock, heat through and taste, adding a little more salt and 1 tsp of ground coriander if you think it needs it (I usually do).

Stir in the chopped coriander and serve with a sprinkle of the ground spices on top.

* The spice grinder I use comes from a South African company called Cape Herb & Spice, and is available from good delis or www.saffronwharf.com.

Best beer match A pale ale or bitter will work well with this or you could drink a Czech lager.

Baked beer & chicory soup with Maroilles croutons

This is a slightly less complicated version of a fabulous soup I tasted several years ago at Jean-Christophe Novelli's restaurant Maison Novelli in Clerkenwell, London. It included a poached egg, which you can, of course, add to each bowl as you serve this soup.

serves 6

5 tbsp sunflower or other light cooking oil

40g butter

6 heads of chicory (endive) – about 700g in total, trimmed
  and halved lengthways

1 onion, peeled and thinly sliced

1 tbsp unrefined caster sugar

1 litre of strong beef stock or stock made with 2 organic
  beef stock cubes

250ml strong northern French beer, such as Jenlain,
  or Belgian brown beer

sea salt and freshly ground black pepper, to taste

1 Maroilles cheese

6 thin slices of sourdough bread, baked hard
  (as in crostini recipe on page 54)

You will need a large, shallow casserole dish

Preheat the oven to 180°C/350°F/Gas 4.

Heat a large frying pan, add 2 tbsp of oil, heat for
a minute, then add the butter. When the foaming
dies down, lay half the halved chicory heads in the
pan. Lightly brown on each side and transfer to
the casserole. Add a little more oil and about 1/3 of
the butter, and fry the rest of the chicory. Add that
to the casserole, too.

Fry the sliced onion briefly in the remaining oil and
butter, and add to the casserole dish. Sprinkle with
the sugar. Deglaze the pan with 3–4 tbsp of the stock
and pour over the vegetables, then bake for about
40–45 minutes until the chicory is nicely caramelized.

Heat the stock and pour it over the vegetables along
with the beer. Cover the pan and return to the oven
for another 45–50 minutes, turning the heat down to
170°C/325°F/Gas 3 after 10 minutes. Check the
seasoning of the soup, adding salt and pepper to taste.

Turn off the oven and turn on the grill. Cut the rind
off the Maroilles and slice thinly. Lay the slices over the
croutons and lay them on the surface of the soup. (If
the Maroilles is very soft, simply spread it over the
croutons.) Place the casserole under the grill and cook
until the cheese has melted and browned.

**Best beer match One of those dishes that goes
really well with the same beer you use to make
the soup, i.e. a northern French bière de garde,
or a Belgian ale.**

" It's not surprising that the northern French from the Pas-de-Calais region, just over the
border from Belgium, are beer rather than wine drinkers. Beers in the region tend to come
under the catch-all title bière de garde, which literally translates as 'a beer to keep' but
includes such contrasting styles as blonde, ambrée and brune. Widely available brands are
Ch'Ti, Jenlain and La Chouffe. "

Mushroom & mustard soup

A blissfully smooth, intensely mushroomy soup that's the perfect match for a dark Trappist beer. You decide how creamy you want it – I prefer to add just a dash to the soup, then swirl a little in each bowl to decorate.

serves 3–4

50g butter

250g portabello mushrooms, wiped clean and roughly chopped

1 small onion (about 90–100g), peeled and chopped

1 clove of garlic, peeled and crushed

1 small potato (about 75g), peeled and finely sliced

1 tbsp madeira

500ml fresh beef stock or stock made with a beef stock cube (or 2 level tsp yeast extract if you're a veggie)

1 rounded tsp grain mustard

2 tbsp double cream (optional) + extra cream for swirling

a good squeeze of lemon

sea salt and freshly ground black pepper, to taste

chopped chervil or parsley, to garnish

Heat a large saucepan or cast iron casserole for a minute or two, add the butter, then, as soon as it's melted, tip in the mushrooms. Stir and cook for about 8–10 minutes until any liquid created begins to evaporate.

Add the onion, stir and fry for 3–4 minutes, then stir in the garlic and fry for a minute longer. Add the potato, stir, then add the madeira and beef stock, and bring to the boil. Simmer until the potato is cooked (about 12–15 minutes).

Remove from the heat and cool for a few minutes, then add the mustard. Pass the soup through a strainer, saving the liquid, and put the mushrooms into a blender. Whizz until smooth, then add half of the reserved liquid and whizz again. Add the remaining liquid and whizz.

Pour the soup back into the pan or casserole. Pour 150ml of water into the blender to pick up the remaining soup you haven't managed to scrape out and add to the pan. Add the cream, if using, then reheat gently without boiling.

Season with a good squeeze of lemon, a little salt and freshly ground black pepper. Garnish each portion with a swirl or splosh of cream, and sprinkle over a little chopped chervil or parsley.

Best beer match We found Westmalle Dubbel was a great match with this soup but you could also try it with a porter or stout.

Chunky potato, onion & cabbage soup with Lancashire cheese

A homely soup that's perfect for a chilly autumn or winter's day.

serves 2

2 tbsp sunflower or light olive oil

15g butter

2 medium onions, peeled and cut into thin slices

1 clove of garlic, peeled and finely sliced
(optional)

2 medium potatoes, peeled and cut into thin
slices

600ml light vegetable stock made with 2 tsp of
organic vegetable stock powder

a handful of finely shredded green cabbage,
spring greens or chard leaves (about 75g)

40–50g mature Lancashire cheese, rind removed
and finely sliced

freshly ground black pepper, to taste

Heat the oil in a large lidded pan or casserole Add the butter, then tip in the onions and garlic, if using. Stir well, turn the heat right down and put a lid on the pan.

Cook, stirring occasionally, for about 10–15 minutes until the onions are completely soft. Add the potato to the pan, pour in the stock and bring to the boil. Simmer uncovered for another 20 minutes, adding the shredded cabbage about 5 minutes before the cooking time is up. Check the seasoning, adding pepper to taste.

Serve in warm soup bowls with 4 or 5 fine slices of cheese arranged over the top. Stir the cheese in before you eat.

Best beer match A good gutsy British ale.

Nuts & other nibbles

Anything salty, crunchy and crispy is good with a beer. It's great if it's cheesy as well. Obviously, you're more likely to buy your nuts and nibbles ready-made but here are a couple of recipes that are well worth rustling up if you're in the mood.

Honey-spiced nuts
This is more a suggestion than a recipe but it makes everyone think you've taken a huge amount of trouble. Which, of course, you haven't. The essential elements are something sweet, like sugar or honey, some kind of spice mix and salt, but you can play around with that pretty much as you like.

serves 4–6

1 tbsp light cooking oil
200g mixed shelled unsalted nuts
1 tbsp clear honey
1–2 tsp Jerk or Cajun seasoning or other hot spice mix
a little sea salt and freshly ground black pepper,
  if needed

Heat a medium-sized frying pan, add the oil and allow to heat through. Tip in the nuts and stir. Drizzle over the honey and sprinkle with 1–1½ tsp of the spice mix (depending how hot it is) and stir-fry over a moderate heat for 2–3 minutes. Check the seasoning, adding a little more spice mix, salt or pepper if you think it needs it. Set aside the nuts until cool.

Best beer match Either a golden ale or strong golden lager.

Paul's cracking cheese straws
(*Illustrated right*) This is the best cheese straw recipe I've ever tasted. It comes from Paul Hayes, who was the first chef at Will's pub, The Marquess. Cut them long as illustrated so that a) everyone knows they're home-made and b) you can fit them in a beer tankard.

serves 6–8

150g plain flour
¼ tsp cayenne pepper
¼ tsp English mustard powder
a pinch of sea salt
100g chilled, unsalted butter, cut into cubes
150g strong, mature farmhouse cheddar,
  coarsely grated
1 egg yolk
2 tbsp water

Sift the flour with the cayenne pepper, mustard and salt and tip into a bowl.
  Cut the butter into the bowl and rub through the flour with your fingertips, as if you were making pastry. Add the cheese and rub in thoroughly. Beat the egg yolk with the water and add just enough to the mix to enable you to pull it together and shape into a flat disc. Wrap in clingfilm and refrigerate for 30 minutes, then take out and allow to come back to room temperature. Preheat the oven to 190°C/375°F/Gas 5.
  Roll out the dough thinly, then cut into long strips about 30cm in length. (Don't cut off the uneven ends – that's what makes them look home-made!) Lay the strips carefully on a couple of lightly oiled baking sheets and bake for about 12–15 minutes until golden brown. Leave on the trays for 10 minutes then transfer them carefully to a wire rack to finish cooling. Eat fresh, ideally, but they will keep well for a couple of days in an airtight tin, and you can refresh them briefly in the oven.

Best beer match There's nothing to beat a good British bitter with these.

Dips & spreads

These recipes are pretty well interchangeable as dips or spreads – it all depends on how thick or sloppy you choose to make them.

Liptauer cheese spread
This is an Austro-Hungarian spread, rather than a German one, but it goes particularly well with Bavarian, helles-style lager.

serves 6–8

110g soft butter

225g curd cheese

2 tbsp soured cream or crème fraîche

1 tsp Dijon mustard

1 tsp paprika + extra for garnish
¼ tsp crushed caraway seeds

2 tbsp finely chopped onion

2 tbsp finely chopped sweet-sour pickled
  cucumber

1 tbsp capers, rinsed and finely chopped

sea salt and freshly ground black pepper, to taste

Beat the butter until soft and creamy, then work in the curd cheese and soured cream or crème fraîche.

Mix in the mustard, paprika and caraway seeds, then fold in the chopped onion, pickled cucumber and capers. Add a little of the juice from the pickled cucumber jar to get a soft but still spreadable consistency.

Check the seasoning, adding salt and pepper to taste, cover and leave in the fridge to mellow for at least two hours.

Sift over a little extra paprika before serving with rye bread or a dark bread like pumpernickel.

Best beer match A Bavarian helles-style or a Czech golden lager.

Beetroot & cream cheese spread

Beetroot makes the most gorgeous-looking spread that really stands out in a selection of dips and spreads.

250g freshly roasted, peeled beetroot or cooked (but not pickled) beets
100g curd or cream cheese
1 large clove of garlic, peeled and chopped, and ½ tsp sea salt (or 1 tsp fresh garlic paste)
1 level tsp ground cumin
3 heaped tbsp finely chopped fresh coriander

Cut the beetroot into cubes and whizz in a food processor until smooth, adding 1 tbsp of cheese if it's hard to get going. Add the remainder of the cheese and whizz again.

Pound the garlic with the salt with a mortar and pestle until it forms a paste, then add to the beetroot mixture along with the cumin. Whizz again. Tip into a bowl and fold in 2 tbsp of chopped coriander. Scatter the rest of the coriander over the top just before serving.

This goes well with light or dark rye bread and wedges of sweet and sour pickled cucumber.

Best beer match A Polish lager or a German Pilsener or Kölsch.

Green & Red's guacamole

Authentic Mexican guacamole is rough and chunky rather than smooth. This recipe comes from Will's Mexican bar Green & Red. Note the tip about the stones.

4 ripe avocados
2 ripe plum tomatoes, de-seeded and finely chopped
1 medium white onion, peeled and finely chopped
1 good handful of fresh coriander, finely chopped
juice of 2 limes
3 green serrano chillies de-seeded and finely chopped
sea salt, to taste

Halve and scoop the flesh out of the avocados and place in a large mixing bowl. Using a potato masher, break down the avocado into a rough pulp. Add all the other ingredients and mix well. Season with salt, then return one or two of the avocado stones to your guacamole to help the colour hold (obviously removing them before serving).

✳ If you refrigerate the guacamole, cover it closely with clingfilm and take it from the fridge at least half an hour before serving to allow the full flavour to come through.

Best beer match A Michelada (see page 173) would be great with this or a light Mexican beer like Dos Equis.

Clockwise from bottom left: chorizo con papas (potatoes), guacamole (see page 23), albondigas (meatballs) and salsa Mexicana. Perfect snacks for serving with a light refreshing beer.

All cold meats are great with beer, whether they're the next-day remains of the Sunday roast, a leftover sausage or two sneakily pinched from the fridge when you arrive home at 2 am, or a posh foie gras terrine or duck liver parfait – great with a saison or Belgian tripel ale.

French-style chicken liver pâté with cognac   *(Illustrated left)*

Well, there's not a lot of cognac in this recipe, if truth be told, but just enough to give it that extra pizazz.

225g fresh, free-range chicken livers

100g butter at room temperature + an extra
  25g for the topping

1 medium onion, peeled and finely chopped

1 large clove of garlic, peeled and finely chopped

4 fresh bay leaves

a couple of sprigs of fresh thyme

1 tbsp cognac or other brandy

sea salt, freshly ground black pepper and
  a pinch of allspice, to taste

a few black peppercorns for decoration
  (optional)

Pick through the chicken livers, cutting away any bits of sinew or greenish patches, and cut into cubes.

Heat 25g of the butter in a saucepan, add the chopped onion and garlic, and cook gently for about 5 minutes until they are soft. Add one of the bay leaves, the thyme and the chicken livers, turn up the heat and fry, stirring for about 3 minutes until the chicken livers are browned on all sides. Take the pan off the heat and cool. Remove the bay leaf and thyme, and tip the livers, onion and garlic into a food processor. Whizz until smooth, then add another 75g of butter, cut into cubes, and whizz again. Season with salt, pepper and a pinch of allspice, add the brandy and whizz again.

Transfer the pâté to a small pot and smooth over the surface. Heat the remaining butter gently and spoon off the milky layer that rises to the surface. Pour the clear butter over the surface of the pâté and decorate with the remaining bay leaves and peppercorns, if using.

Transfer the pâté to the fridge for at least a couple of hours, then return to room temperature before serving with plain or melba toast (thick slices of bread, toasted, then cut in half horizontally and the exposed sides grilled to create deliciously thin, crispy toast).

Best beer match This is a very beer-friendly recipe but it goes particularly well with strong pale ales like Anchor Liberty and American IPAs. Try it with a Belgian tripel, too.

Ham & parsley pâté   This delicate, very English-tasting spread is the perfect way to use up the remains of a boiled gammon or bacon joint – or you can make it from scratch with good-quality dry cured ham.

serves 6

140g cooked smoked ham

150g unsalted butter at room temperature

1½–2 tsp English or Dijon mustard

3 heaped tbsp finely chopped parsley

1 heaped tbsp finely snipped chives

white pepper and sea salt, to taste

Chop the ham up roughly and process in a food processor until finely chopped. Dice the butter, add it to the ham and process until smooth. Add mustard to taste and enough water to make a spreadable consistency.

Transfer the pâté to a bowl, and stir in the parsley and chives. Season with white pepper and a little salt, if you feel it needs it (it may not if the ham is salty).

Refrigerate for an hour or two to allow the flavours to develop, then allow to come back to room temperature before serving with either crusty fresh bread or toast.

Best beer match Ideal with English bitter such as White Horse Bitter, a summer beer like Hop Back Summer Lightning or a honey-flavoured beer like Young's Waggle Dance.

ultimate roast beef sandwich on ciabatta | hand-carved ham & piccalilli on granary

Sandwiches

Beer and sandwiches were Labour prime minister Harold Wilson's legendary solution to industrial relations problems – and with good reason. They make a fine, satisfying meal. Or they should do – sandwiches made from rubbery sliced bread with a meagre filling, served with a gassy lager, are not much cop at all. We like our sandwiches made with doorstep-thick slices hand-cut from a proper artisanal-baked loaf, crammed with filling so that you have to use two hands to pick them up.

We want hand-carved ham and piccalilli on granary (see above) with our freshly pulled pint of bitter, some freshly grilled veg and goats' cheese on sourdough (see opposite, right) with our witbier, and some really crispy dry-cured bacon in our BLT or chicken club, which we plan to drink with a golden ale or lager. Is that a lot to ask? The following are three rather more ambitious sandwich ideas that you might enjoy.

Ultimate roast beef sandwich (*Illustrated above*) You can use leftover roast beef for
this but part of what makes the sandwich ultimate is using freshly cooked beef with its warm roasting juices.

serves 4

1 small (about 800–850g) topside roasting joint, roasted
  rare and cooled for about 45 minutes
2 ready-to-bake ciabattas or other long, flat loaves
a small jar of creamed horseradish sauce
a small pack of fresh rocket or watercress
freshly ground black pepper, to taste

Slice the beef as thinly as possible with a sharp knife. Cut each ciabatta or loaf in half lengthways and lightly toast on both sides.

Arrange the sliced beef over the cut side of the bottom halves. Spread generously with horseradish

sauce, spoon over the juices that are left in the roasting pan and grind over a little black pepper. Top with the rocket or watercress leaves. Press down the top half of each ciabatta or loaf firmly and divide it into two or three.

**Best beer match A good British bitter like
Timothy Taylor's Landlord.**

pastrami on rye with dill cucumbers

grilled vegetables & goats' cheese on sourdough

Pastrami on rye (*Illustrated above*) A classic New York deli-style sandwich.

serves 2

6 long thin slices of freshly baked light rye or
  sourdough bread

120g pack sliced pastrami

3–4 large pickled dill cucumbers, sliced

about 3 tbsp Dijonnaise (mayo mixed with
  Dijon mustard)

butter or butter-style spread

Spread one side of each slice of bread thinly with
butter or spread, then top three of the slices with the
pastrami and sliced pickled cucumbers. Spread the
Dijonnaise over the other slices and press down well.
Halve each sandwich and serve.

Best beer match   A Pilsener.

Roasted Red Leicester, red onion & sweet pickle sandwich

This is an easy way of making toasted sandwiches for a crowd, though you could equally well use the same
combination of ingredients to make a conventional toasted sandwich.

serves 3–4

1 small round pain de campagne or other small, flattish
  rustic loaf

75g sweet, fruity chutney (not Branston's for this one)

1 small to medium red onion, finely sliced into rings

100g Red Leicester cheese, grated

1 tbsp sunflower or light olive oil

Preheat the oven to 200°C/400°F/Gas 6.

   Cut across the loaf horizontally so that you have two
equal halves. Spread the chutney on the bottom half,

then add a layer of finely sliced onion rings (leave out
the thicker end pieces) and top with the grated cheese.
Press the top half of the loaf down firmly on top.

   Grease a large sheet of foil with the oil and wrap
carefully around the filled loaf, then bake for 20–25
minutes until the crust is crisp and the cheese is all
melted and gooey. Cut into wedges and serve.

**Best beer match   A good hearty ale like
Young's Special.**

Kebabs

Kebabs and lager are, of course, a takeaway classic but have you ever wondered why it works? Normally with grilled meat you'd think of drinking a more substantial ale but the salad accompaniments, particularly the raw onion and lemon, make a light lager or Pilsener much more refreshing. Turkey and Cyprus have a couple of their own, which actually aren't at all bad (see Best beer match below).

(Almost) doner kebabs

This is the nearest I reckon you can get to an authentic doner kebab if there's no Turkish restaurant handy. Hugely popular with adults and children alike.

serves 4–8

1 small to medium sized onion peeled, quartered
  and roughly chopped
500g extra lean minced beef
500g minced lamb
2 large cloves of garlic
1 level tsp ground coriander
1 level tsp ground cumin
3 tbsp finely chopped fresh coriander leaves
3 tbsp finely chopped fresh parsley
2 tbsp finely chopped fresh mint
sea salt and freshly ground black pepper, to taste
3–4 tbsp light olive oil
a little flour for dusting

for the chickpea, garlic and yoghurt dressing:

1 x 170g tub of hummus
2 tbsp natural yoghurt
1 tbsp lemon juice
1 large clove of garlic, crushed

to serve:

2 packs of pitta breads
shredded iceberg lettuce leaves
2 lemons cut into quarters
1 mild onion, finely sliced

The meat mixture is best made in a food processor but you may have to do it in two batches. Place the onion in the bowl of a food processor and pulse until finely chopped. Add the minced beef and lamb, garlic, ground coriander, cumin, fresh herbs and salt and pepper, and process until all the seasonings are well amalgamated and the mixture is almost like a paste in texture. Leave for half an hour for the flavours to amalgamate.

Meanwhile, mix the hummus with the yoghurt, lemon juice and garlic. Check the seasoning, then pour into a bowl and refrigerate.

Divide the meat mixture into 16 portions. With lightly floured hands, roll each portion into a ball then, with the heel of your hand, press each one down firmly to create a flattish disc. Heat a ridged grill pan or non-stick frying pan for about 2–3 minutes until really hot, then brush the meat patties lightly in oil and fry them in batches. Press them down firmly with a wooden spatula as you cook them until they're well browned on each side and thoroughly cooked through (about 1 minute each side). Set aside and keep warm.

Warm the pitta breads through briefly in a toaster or under a low grill, keeping them covered on a plate with a tea towel so they stay warm and don't go hard.

Put the lettuce leaves in a bowl and lay out the lemon wedges, sliced onion and chickpea dressing. Split the pitta breads and fill each one with one or two meat patties, plus whatever other fillings each person fancies. For the full monty, go for a dollop of dip or a squeeze of lemon juice, a few slices of onion and a few lettuce leaves.

Best beer match When we were road-testing this recipe with beer, we found that Efes Turkish and Keo Cypriot Pilseners were pretty good matches. But obviously any Pilsener would do the job.

" I was impressed by the information on the Turkish beer company Efes's website that 'Efes heroes travel a lot, do extreme sports, study architecture and lie on an ocean beach in a (sic) good company, with a glass of Efes beer in hand, watching the sun go down', although the extreme sports and architecture link seems a bit tenuous. Apparently, rice is included in the brewing process. "

Cheese tarts & pies

Cheese and pastry always make a great beer match, but even though these recipes contain pretty much the same ingredients, they couldn't be more different.

Alsace-style onion tart

(Illustrated left) A particularly delicious tart with a French, rather than an English, flavour. It's slightly easier to fry the onions in two frying pans.

6 medium onions, peeled and thinly sliced
4 tbsp olive oil
25g butter
250g ready-made or home-made shortcrust pastry
3 large or 4 medium free-range eggs, lightly beaten
250g crème fraîche
40g grated Gruyère or Comté cheese
sea salt, freshly ground black pepper and freshly
  grated nutmeg, to taste
You will need a 23cm diameter flan tin

Heat two frying pans over a medium heat, add half the oil to each and then half the butter. Tip half the onions into each pan, stir well, then leave over a low to moderate heat until soft and golden, stirring the onions occasionally. Set aside and cool.

Preheat the oven to 200°C/400°F/Gas 6. Roll the pastry out into a circle big enough to fit the flan tin. Lower the pastry into the tin, trim any overhanging edges and lightly prick the base with the prongs of a fork. Line with a piece of foil or greaseproof paper, weighed down with some baking beans, and bake the pastry shell for about 12 minutes.

Remove the paper and beans, and return the pastry case to the oven for another 3 minutes. Brush a little of the beaten egg over the base of the part-cooked pastry case and return to the oven for a couple of minutes more. Reduce the heat to 190°C/375°F/Gas 5. Mix the remaining beaten egg with the crème fraîche and grated Gruyère or Comté, and season with salt, pepper and a little freshly grated nutmeg. Tip the onions into the tart and carefully pour the egg mixture over the top, making sure that it is distributed evenly.

Put the flan tin on a baking sheet and bake for about 30 minutes until the top is puffed up and lightly browned. Cool for about 10 minutes before serving.

Best beer match An obvious pairing would be an Alsace lager like Kronenbourg 1664. More interesting would be a blonde ale like Fischer Tradition or Grimbergen Blonde.

Cheese, onion & potato pie

Like a glorious, giant cheese and onion pasty, this is perfect football match-watching fodder.

serves 6
2 x 375g pack ready-rolled puff pastry
1 large mild onion, peeled and finely sliced
225g matured farmhouse Cheddar, thinly sliced
2 medium to large potatoes, peeled and finely sliced
1 medium free-range egg, lightly beaten
freshly ground black pepper, to taste
You will need a lightly oiled rectangular baking sheet

Preheat the oven to 220C°/425°F/Gas 7.

Take the pastry out of the fridge 10–15 minutes before you intend to use it. Remove one piece and place it on the baking sheet, trimming the ends if necessary. Put a layer of sliced onion over the base, leaving about a 2cm border round the edges. Top with a layer of cheese, then a layer of potato, seasoning each layer lightly as you go.

Repeat the layers, finishing with cheese. Roll the other piece of pastry so that it's big enough to cover the base and the filling. Brush the edges of the pastry lightly with the beaten egg, then carefully lower the top onto the pie without overstretching it, pressing it down well at the edges. Trim and knock up the edges of the pie and cut three vertical slits in the top. Brush with the beaten egg.

Bake in the preheated oven for 20 minutes, then reduce the heat to 190°C/375°F/Gas 5 for another 30–40 minutes until well browned and cooked through. Leave to cool for at least 20 minutes before serving.

Best beer match A robust, fruity British ale such as Marston's Double Drop, or an American or American-style IPA.

margherita

basil pesto & olives

Pizza

Beer and pizza. We love it. It's not when we drink our most memorable beers but when we just want to relax.

Do I always make my own pizza? No, just occasionally, then wonder why I don't do it more often – it's so simple and so good. But time is short and there are so many excellent ready-made pizzas around now. What I tend to do, though, is to buy a very basic margherita pizza and dress it up. You can then choose your own toppings, which tend to be of better quality than shop-bought ones.

We like strong, punchy flavours like anchovies, olives and hot peppers (all very beer friendly) but you can equally well use fresh peppers, mushrooms, bacon,

salami, chorizo and pepperoni, or seafood, like prawns and tuna. Raw onion or finely sliced spring onions add an edge, as does a little fresh rocket scattered over the pizza a couple of minutes before the end of the cooking period, drizzled with olive oil, then put back in the oven for a couple of minutes to wilt.

You can also vary the cheese – I like to add Taleggio (see below) which I find has more flavour than most mozzarella you can buy. Goats' cheese is also good, especially with broccoli (which you should steam lightly first). Just use your imagination…

Bacon, artichoke & Taleggio pizza This makes a sophisticated topping if you're looking to impress friends. Don't worry if you can't get hold of '00' flour – you can use strong bread flour instead.

makes 2 large pizzas serving 2–3 each
for the dough:
150g strong white flour
125g Italian '00' flour
½ level tsp fine sea salt
1 level tsp quick-acting yeast
2 tbsp olive oil
about 175ml hand-hot water
fine semolina for dusting the baking tray

for the topping:
1 tbsp light cooking oil
200g bacon lardons or diced pancetta
400ml home-made or good-quality, shop-bought Italian passata *
8–10 grilled artichokes in oil or a 280g jar of sliced artichokes
225g Taleggio cheese, rinded and finely sliced
olive oil for topping
You will need two large rectangular baking trays, preferably non-stick

pepperoni   onions & anchovies

Sift the two flours into a bowl, together with the salt and yeast. Mix together, then form a hollow in the centre. Add the olive oil and half the warm water, and stir to incorporate the flour. Gradually add as much of the remaining water as you need to pull the dough together – it should take most of it because you need a wettish dough.

Turn the dough onto a board and knead for 10 minutes until smooth and elastic, adding a little extra flour to prevent the dough sticking, if you need to. Put the dough into a lightly oiled bowl, cover with clingfilm and leave in a warm place to double in size (about 1–1¼ hours). Meanwhile, heat 1 tbsp oil in a medium-sized frying pan and fry the bacon lardons for 3–4 minutes until they start to brown.

Preheat the oven to its maximum setting. Knock the dough down and divide in half. Pull and shape one piece of dough into a large rectangle, then place it on a dusted baking tray and push it out towards the edges of the tray – it doesn't have to be even. Spread half the passata over the top, then scatter over half

the lardons and sliced artichokes. Distribute half the cheese over the top.

Repeat with the other piece of dough and the remaining topping ingredients. Drizzle a little olive oil over the top of the two pizzas and bake for 8–10 minutes until the dough has puffed up and the cheese has browned.

* To make home-made passata, heat 2 tbsp of olive oil in a large frying pan or wok, add 1 clove of crushed garlic, fry for a few seconds, then add 1 level tbsp of tomato paste. Tip in 500g chopped, skinned, fresh tomatoes and stir well. Cover for 5 minutes to soften the tomatoes, then break them down with a fork or wooden spoon and simmer uncovered for a further 5 minutes until the mixture is thick and pulpy. Season with pepper and a little salt, and cool.

Best beer match A light Pilsener like Peroni Nastro Azzurro is perfect with pizza.

" My family are all football nuts. When the World Cup is on, I love to lay on some themed beers and snacks when we watch a match together, like jamon serrano and chorizo with San Miguel when we're playing Spain, or pizza and Peroni if it's Italy... "

pasta, antipasti & risotto

Where would we all be without pasta? It's hard to contemplate a week or, if you're Italian, a day without it, yet the fact has to be faced that it's more natural to accompany it – and antipasti – with wine than with beer. This state of affairs is tacitly acknowledged by most books on beer and food, which rarely have a chapter on Italian recipes.

Why? Well, the majority of pasta sauces are based on cooked tomatoes, which generally pair better with sharp dry drinks such as dry white wine, or Italian reds like chianti or valpolicella, which have a pronounced degree of acidity. Most beers aren't acid, many are malty and some are quite sweet, none of which are characteristics you normally look for in a pairing with pasta, or with risotto, come to that.

However, all is not lost, as many beer-loving Italophiles will testify. You can either pick your beer carefully to match your dish or tweak your pasta sauce, as I've done in the following recipes, to make it more beer-friendly (remember it's the sauce you match, not the pasta).

You can find our specific recommendations for different types of pasta sauces on page 41, but as a general rule:

* Lighter pasta dishes and risottos based on creamy sauces or containing seafood or spring vegetables are best with lighter, more refreshing beers like Pilseners, Kölsch, light lagers and American-style pale ales.

* More robust, rustic pasta dishes with meat, dark mushroom or aubergine-based sauces work better with richly flavoured amber ales or lagers.

* Risottos made with strongly flavoured ingredients such as porcini, beetroot and radicchio (a bitter, red endive) also pair well with beer.

Antipasti & other Italian dishes

In contrast to some Italian dishes, antipasti – the cold meats and salads that the Italians generally serve before pasta – are really good with beer.

Reason? Cured meats, such as salami, have a fair proportion of fat. The vegetables, like sundried tomatoes or marinated mushrooms, are often preserved or served with a sharp, acidic dressing.

Some vegetables, such as artichokes, and ingredients, such as anchovies, are actually easier to pair with beer (we like a Pilsener or a Kölsch) than they are with wine. Eating antipasti is actually incredibly easy, whether or not you have pasta afterwards. You can buy practically everything you need from the deli counter of a reasonably-sized supermarket or – even better – from an Italian deli.

So far as main courses are concerned, the natural instinct is, again, to pour a glass of red wine. However, the Italian way of cooking meat like chicken, veal, lamb and even steak over an open fire actually suits beer pretty well.

We find that amber ales and French ambrée beers are generally the best types of beer to drink with Mediterranean food, including Italian. They also go well with substantial dishes such as bollito misto (mixed boiled meats, served with pungent mustardy mostarda di cremona) and lentils and sausages, such as cotechino.

" Bits and bobs on different plates, and beers to match – this is my absolutely favourite way of eating, and it's popular pretty much throughout Europe. Beer, especially lager, which is the prevalent beer in Italy, is amazingly versatile and goes with an incredible range of flavours. Beer also matches one other crucial part of the eating and drinking experience: the weather. Nothing beats a strong-flavoured beer on a cold day, except possibly an ice-cold beer on a hot one! That is, I believe, one of the crucial reasons beer styles are as they are in each country. "

Match the sauce, not the pasta

It stands to reason, when you think about it, that when you're trying to find a beer to partner a pasta dish (or a dish based on an essentially neutral meat like chicken), the starting point should not be the type of pasta but the sauce. For example, you'd want a different style of beer to partner a creamy spaghetti carbonara from the beer you'd choose for a lasagne or spaghetti and meatballs.

There are also ingredients you can add to pasta dishes to make them more beer-friendly. These include garlic, olives, capers and sun-dried tomatoes (good with seafood-based pastas); mature Parmesan and smoked bacon or pancetta (which will make cream sauces more savoury); and roasted or grilled vegetables, especially butternut squash, cooked dried beans such as borlotti beans, and chestnuts.

Here are some popular sauces and pasta fillings, together with the beers that we think go with them best. For gnocchi and polenta dishes, follow similar guidelines, though bear in mind that polenta, which normally incorporates butter and Parmesan, tends to be considerably richer than pasta.

* Cooked tomato-based sauces e.g. spaghetti napoli
Viennese-style lager, amber ale

* Creamy sauces (including light mushroom-based sauces) e.g. spaghetti carbonara (with bacon), fettucine alfredo (with cheese)
Light to strong golden lager

* Light vegetable sauces e.g. pasta primavera (with spring vegetables)
Light Pilsener

* Ravioli or cannelloni with spinach and ricotta
Light Pilsener or lager

* Dark mushroom-based sauces or sauces made with dried mushrooms such as porcini
Belgian bruin/brune beer or dunkel weisse

* Seafood sauces e.g. spaghetti alle vongole (with clams), linguine with crab
Pilsener, Kölsch, witbier

* Cheese sauces e.g. quattro formaggi, gorgonzola, macaroni cheese
Viennese lager, amber ale; traditional British ale with macaroni cheese

* Pesto sauces
Golden/blonde ale, lager

* Meaty sauces e.g. bolognese and baked pasta dishes like lasagne
Amber ales and lagers or blonde ales if added to the sauce (see page 43); sauces with chicken livers are good with an American IPA

* Spicy sauces e.g. spaghetti aglio olio e peperoncino (with garlic, oil and hot peppers), penne all'arrabbiata (with tomato and dried chillies)
Light lager or Pilsener

* Piquant sauces e.g. puttanesca (with olives, capers and anchovies)
Strong dark Trappist ale

" Typically, Italian beers like Peroni Nastro Azzuro are pale, Pilsener-style beers, relatively neutral in flavour and served with pizza or drunk on their own. But there are a few brave souls stemming the tide. The Associazione Culturale Unionbirrai is a collective of micro-brewers, brewpubs and beer enthusiasts that promotes real ale and other craft beers (birra artigianale). Members include Baladin in Milan, Birrificio Italiano near the Swiss border and Birrificio Babb in Manerbio. "

Smoky bacon bolognese

Adding bacon to a bolognese definitely makes it more beer-friendly. If you don't eat bacon, double the amount of smoked pimentón.

serves 4

2 tbsp olive oil

100g smoked streaky bacon, chopped, or diced smoked pancetta

1 medium onion, peeled and finely chopped

450g lean minced beef

1 large clove of garlic, peeled and finely chopped

1 tsp sweet smoked pimentón (mild Spanish paprika)

1 x 400g tin whole or chopped tomatoes

175ml blonde Belgian beer e.g. Leffe Blonde

400g spaghetti

sea salt and freshly ground black pepper, to taste

freshly grated Parmesan cheese or Grana Padano
  (a Parmesan-style cheese), to serve

Heat 1 tbsp of oil in a large frying pan, add the bacon and fry for a minute or two until the fat starts to run. Add the onion, stir, turn the heat down and cook for another 7–8 minutes until the onion is soft. Scoop the onion and bacon out of the pan with a slotted spoon and set aside.

Turn the heat back up and brown half the meat. Remove from the pan, pour off any liquid, then brown the remaining meat. Tip the bacon, onion and mince back into the pan, stir in the garlic and pimentón and cook for a minute, then add the tomatoes, breaking them down with a wooden spoon or fork. Pour in the beer, stir, turn the heat down low and simmer for 15–20 minutes, stirring occasionally.

Meanwhile, cook the spaghetti until al dente in plenty of boiling water. Drain, reserving a little of the cooking water, return to the pan and toss with the remaining oil. Add 2 tbsp of the cooking water to the bolognese sauce and season with salt and black pepper.

Serve the spaghetti in large shallow bowls with the sauce spooned on top. Sprinkle with grated Parmesan or Grana Padano.

Best beer match **You could carry on drinking Leffe Blonde or another blonde Belgian ale, or switch to an amber ale or lager.**

" People are sometimes a bit sniffy about blonde beers, which aren't recognized as a beer category, but I see them as the beer world's equivalent of chardonnay – a great way to get sceptics into beer. The term simply means a pale- to golden-coloured beer, but has become recognized as a distinctive style of abbey or Trappist beer such as Leffe, French bière de garde and American ale. These well-balanced beers are characterized by a mild malty taste with a subtle sweet fruitiness and light hop bitterness. "

Roast butternut squash, chestnut & wild mushroom fusilli

An elaborate but fabulous vegetarian pasta dish for a special occasion. You can cut down on the work by using ready-peeled chestnuts but freshly roasted ones do taste wonderful.

serves 4 or 6 as a starter

1 medium to large butternut squash (about 800g)
4 tbsp olive oil
350g fresh chestnuts or 200g ready-prepared cooked chestnuts
30g dried chanterelles or other dried mushrooms
250ml warm vegetable stock made with 1 tsp vegetable bouillon powder
1 medium onion, peeled and roughly chopped
25g butter
1 large clove of garlic, peeled and crushed
1/2 tsp sweet smoked pimentón or mild paprika
2 tbsp madeira, sweet sherry or tawny port
325g fusilli or other dried pasta shapes
sea salt and freshly ground black pepper, to taste
fresh Parmesan cheese, to serve

Preheat the oven to 220°C/425°F/Gas 7. Quarter the butternut squash and scoop out the seeds. Cut each quarter into 3 or 4 pieces and cut away the skin with a sharp knife. Put the squash in a roasting tin, pour over 2 tbsp of the oil, season with salt and pepper, and mix well. Roast for about 30 minutes until the squash is well coloured, shaking the pan occasionally.

Cut a cross in the rounded side of each chestnut with a sharp knife, then lay them out cut-side upwards in a baking tin. Roast at the same temperature as the squash for about 15–20 minutes until they split open, then turn off the oven but leave them in the tin. Take two or three at a time, let them cool a little until you can handle them, then peel off the shell and outer layer of brown papery skin. If they become difficult to peel, simply heat them up again.

Soak the mushrooms for 15 minutes in the warm vegetable stock, then drain and sieve the stock to remove any grit. Heat the remaining oil in a large frying pan or wok and fry the onion over a moderate heat until beginning to brown at the edges. Turn the heat down, add the butter, then, once it has melted, add the crushed garlic and pimentón. Add the mushrooms and stir-fry for a few minutes, then add the madeira and the reserved vegetable stock. Leave to simmer for 5 minutes while you put on the pasta to cook, following the timing on the packet, until al dente.

Roughly chop the peeled chestnuts, add them to the mushroom mixture and continue to cook over a low heat. Cut up the roasted squash into slightly smaller cubes and add to the pan, together with any roasting juices.

Drain the pasta well, reserving some of the cooking water, then tip the pasta into the sauce and toss together thoroughly. Add a little of the reserved pasta cooking water, and check the seasoning, adding salt and pepper to taste.

Serve in warm bowls with some finely shaved or coarsely grated Parmesan.

✳ If you use a non-dairy spread instead of butter and a vegan cheese, this recipe would be suitable for vegans.

Best beer match A very beer-friendly dish that tastes as good with robust English ales, such as Shepherd Neame 1698 and Black Sheep, as it does with an American IPA or brown ale. Harviestoun Schiehallion is also a good match.

Prawn, fennel & leek risotto

The flavour of risotto, like that of pasta, depends more on the flavour of the ingredients that are cooked with the rice than on the rice itself. In general, you need a slightly lighter, drier beer than you would to accompany a comparable pasta dish.

serves 2

1 tbsp olive oil

25g butter

1 small onion or ½ a medium onion, peeled
  and finely chopped

1 small bulb of fennel (about 200g), trimmed
  and finely sliced

150g arborio, carnaroli or vialone nano
  risotto rice

½ a glass (about 75ml) dry white wine

500ml hot fish stock or vegetable stock made
  with 2 level tsp vegetable bouillon powder, mixed
  with 1 tsp Thai fish sauce (nam pla)

1 small leek, trimmed, cleaned and finely sliced

200g fresh or thawed, frozen prawns

1 tbsp finely chopped fresh dill

1 tbsp crème fraîche or double cream (optional)

sea salt, freshly ground black pepper and a squeeze
  of lemon juice, to taste

Heat the oil in a heavy saucepan, add the butter, then, when it has melted, tip in the chopped onion and fennel. Stir, cover and cook gently until soft (about 5 minutes). Remove the lid, turn the heat up a little, tip in the rice, stir and cook for 2–3 minutes until the grains have turned opaque and are beginning to catch on the bottom of the pan. Add the wine, stir and let it bubble up and evaporate. Add the hot stock, a ladleful at a time, whenever the liquid in the risotto is absorbed, stirring it every couple of minutes.

After 10 minutes, add the sliced leek. Keep stirring the risotto and adding stock until it starts to look creamy and the rice is tender but still has a little bite to it (about another 8–10 minutes). Remove from the heat, stir in the prawns (and any liquid that has accumulated under them), the dill and the crème fraîche, if using, cover and leave for 5 minutes.

Season to taste with salt, pepper and a squeeze of lemon juice, then spoon the risotto into warm bowls.

Best beer match We really enjoyed this with Colomba, a light, aromatic Corsican wheat beer. It also works well with Jacobsen's new Bramley Wit and Kasteel Cru.

seafood

If you think of the basic tastes that work well with beer, many of them are found in seafood. Fresh, marine saltiness, the delicate sweetness of fresh shellfish, the oiliness of sardines and mackerel, the fattiness of eel, tuna and salmon all create hooks for beer to latch onto. Deep-fried foods, we already know, are great with beer, and fish has more than its share of those options. Even more delicate dishes like creamy chowders or creamily-sauced fish can work with a Pilsener just as well as with a dry white wine.

The following beers are particularly good with seafood:

* Light but not overly hoppy Pilseners, like Veltlins from Germany, are perfect drunk with simply prepared white fish, such as grilled plaice or sole, or with fish or prawn salads. Kölsch works with these kinds of dishes, too.

* Hoppier Pilseners, like Jever, pair well with pickled and smoked fish.

* Light wheat beers, such as witbiers, suit mussels, crab and Asian-spiced fish dishes like the tuna burgers on page 57.

* Golden lagers and ales, such as Duvel, work well with scallops and richer fish dishes in creamy sauces, especially salmon, as well as with fish pies and fishcakes.

* Sour red ales, like Rodenbach Grand Cru, suit the sort of fish dish that you'd have with a pinot noir – panfried or grilled salmon or tuna, for example. If you're feeling daring, try a raspberry beer.

* Gueuze, especially oude gueuze, pairs well with Belgian-style fish stews and oily fish like sardines and mackerel.

* Dry Irish stouts, like Guinness, are not only a great match for oysters (see page 50) but also for scallops, creamy chowders and smoked fish pies.

* English bitters, such as Harveys Sussex Best Bitter, are just what you need to wash down a portion of fish and chips.

Guinness & oysters

Oysters and Guinness is not only a classic food and beer match but a historic one, stemming from the period some 200 years ago when oysters and porter were staple food and drink for the poor.

The combination works on so many levels. Aesthetic: the dramatic contrast of the opalescent pearly oysters against the dark liquid, their colour echoed in the ivory head at the top of the glass. Texture and temperature: the way the cool, smooth velvety liquid and the silken seawater-infused oysters follow each other, slipping down the throat. The flavour: the briney oysters rounding off the edges of the bitter stout. Pure magic!

Can you pull the same trick with other stouts? Occasionally you get as good a match but it's not as predictably great. Oyster stouts, which you'd obviously expect to work with oysters, tend to have their subtle briney hint knocked out by the oysters. Imperial stouts are too rich, English stouts, such as Mackeson, too sweet. Porters, despite the historic associations, can be a touch bitter, although Robin

Hancock of the Wright Brothers Oyster and Porter House in Borough Market, London, is a big fan of the 1850 London Porter from the Pitfield Brewery, which sells particularly well in their bar.

As for the type of oyster, true aficionados would say that natives are best, but we've enjoyed all kinds with our stout. For pure unadulterated pleasure, it's better not to add anything at all: no lemon, no shallot vinegar, no Tabasco. Nothing but a slice or two of soda bread and some good farmhouse butter.

And what about cooked oysters and Irish stout? Not bad in a creamy chowder or with Oysters Rockefeller, but when the oysters are deep-fried or served Asian-style, we prefer a sparkling Kasteel Cru or a Pilsener.

" **In the early 18th century there was a craze in London pubs for mixing three different ale styles together at a cost of a whopping 4d a pint. In Shoreditch, Ralph Harwood brewed a beer similar in style (dark, bitter, strong) and sold it for 3d a pint. The drink was a huge favourite among the porters of London and the rest is history...** "

Mussels with fennel & witbier *(Illustrated overleaf)*

Anyone who's ever been to Belgium – or to a Belgo restaurant – will have enjoyed those massive kilo helpings of mussels and chips (one overflowing bowl arrives and you think that's your lot, then a second one follows). Beer, especially a Belgian witbier, makes just as good a base to cook them with as white wine. For this recipe, I've picked up the spicing with some extra coriander seeds and some fragrant, aniseedy fennel.

serves 2 as a main course, 4 as a starter

2kg fresh mussels
4 tbsp sunflower or other light oil
1 medium onion, peeled and finely chopped
½ a medium bulb of fennel (about 110g), trimmed
   and finely chopped
1 large clove of garlic, crushed
1 level tsp lightly crushed coriander seeds
150ml witbier, such as Hoegaarden
a few drops of Thai fish sauce (nam pla) – optional
a small handful of fresh parsley, finely chopped
You will need a large, lidded saucepan or casserole

Tip the mussels into a sink of cold water and swirl them around. Move them to a colander. Change the sink water and replace the mussels. Remove any 'beards' with a small, sharp knife and a good yank. Place each one as you finish in a large bowl of water and leave to soak for at least half an hour. Drain them and discard any open ones.

Meanwhile, heat the oil in a large, lidded pan or casserole and cook the finely chopped onion and fennel gently for 10–15 minutes or until soft. Stir in the crushed garlic and coriander, and cook for a further minute. Raise the heat, pour in the witbier and bring it to boiling point. Immediately tip in the mussels, put a lid on the pan and cook over a high heat for 3 minutes, shaking the pan a couple of times.

Take off the lid and check that the mussels are open. If not, replace the lid and cook for another minute. Discard any unopened mussels. Stir in the parsley and check the broth for seasoning, adding a few drops of Thai fish sauce if you want to boost the fishy flavour.

Serve the mussels in large bowls with crusty bread or chips. Provide another large bowl for the empty shells.

Best beer match Drink the same beer as you use to make the dish.

Crab & witbier

This is simply one of the most sublime beer and food combinations. Whether the crab is simply served fresh in a sandwich or salad, or given a spicy Thai twist, it's a sure-fire hit. The citrussy, spicy character of the beer handles ingredients such as lime and chilli to perfection without overwhelming the delicate flavour of the crab. It will also work brilliantly with the fashionable Italian pasta dish linguine with crab. These combinations are guaranteed to win round people who think they don't like beer!

Spicy crab crostini   The perfect accompaniment for a nicely chilled glass of witbier.

makes 12 crostini, enough for 4

150g fresh white crab meat + 1 tbsp brown crab meat
  or mayonnaise

1 spring onion, trimmed and very finely sliced

1 small red or green chilli, de-seeded and very finely
  chopped

grated zest of 1/2 an unwaxed lime

a good squeeze of lime juice

1 heaped tbsp finely chopped fresh coriander
  leaves

sea salt and cayenne pepper, to taste

12 crostini bases *

Pick through the crab meat, removing any bits of shell. Mix with the spring onion, chopped chilli, lime zest, juice and coriander leaves. Add salt and pepper and

extra lime or chilli to taste. Spread onto the crostini bases and serve immediately.

* To make your own crostini bases, preheat the oven to 190°C/375°F/Gas 5. Thinly slice a ready-to-bake ciabatta loaf at a slight slant (to make longer slices) and place on a couple of baking sheets. Spray lightly with olive oil (or trickle a little oil over them) and bake until crisp and lightly browned (about 15 minutes). Cool before using. They'll keep for a couple of days in an airtight tin.

Best beer match Witbier like Celis or Hoegaarden. You could also serve a summer ale, a Pilsener or a ginger-flavoured beer.

Crab, prawn & dill fishcakes

These little fishcakes are particularly useful because they finish off the brown crab meat that you often have left over from recipes that call for only white meat. An added bonus is that they're really easy to make. Serve with a red pepper aioli.

makes 24–26 small fishcakes, enough for 6–8

275g skinless, boneless white fish fillet, such as cod

175g fresh or frozen small peeled prawns (thawed)

150g brown crab meat

1 tsp Thai fish sauce (nam pla)

grated rind of ½ an unwaxed lemon

2 spring onions, trimmed and finely sliced

3 tbsp finely chopped fresh dill

2 level tbsp fine dried breadcrumbs + extra for coating

sunflower or light olive oil for frying

sea salt and cayenne pepper, to taste

Cut the white fish into large chunks. Put in a food processor with the prawns and brown crab meat, and pulse roughly until just combined.

Add the Thai fish sauce, lemon rind, spring onions, dill and 2 tbsp of breadcrumbs and pulse again, leaving the mixture with a bit of texture to it rather than making it smooth. Season with salt and cayenne pepper. Tip some more breadcrumbs into a shallow bowl.

Take tablespoons of the mixture and lightly form them into fishcakes, flattening them slightly. Dip in breadcrumbs and set aside. (You can do this in advance and keep the fishcakes in the fridge.) When you're ready to cook them, heat 4–5 tbsp of oil in a medium-sized frying pan and fry them for about 2 minutes each side until lightly browned.

Best beer match Witbier or weissbier.

Red pepper aioli

1 grilled or roasted red pepper or piquillo pepper
  (about 75g), roughly chopped *

1 small clove of garlic crushed to a paste with
  ½ tsp sea salt

3 tbsp mayonnaise

2 tbsp plain yoghurt

a few drops of Tabasco or other hot sauce

Whizz the red pepper and garlic paste in a blender with the mayonnaise until smooth. Add the yoghurt and whizz again. Add Tabasco to taste.

* It's worth making a batch of grilled and roasted peppers for using in other recipes. To grill the peppers, place them over an open flame until the skin is black, put them in a bowl covered with clingfilm and leave for 10 minutes, then rinse off the skins under cold running water. Remove the seeds and chop the peppers roughly.

Salmon burgers with goats' cheese & sun-dried tomatoes

I got the inspiration for this recipe from browsing around the aisles of Whole Foods Market in Denver during the Great American Beer Festival. For a barbecue, salmon burgers are a great alternative to meat burgers. The Thai tuna burgers are a variation.

serves 3–6, depending on how hungry you are

450g skinless filleted salmon, cut into chunks

80g goats' cheese

4 spring onions, trimmed and finely chopped

80g SunBlush® or other roasted dried tomatoes in oil, finely chopped

a handful of fresh basil leaves

40g natural dried breadcrumbs

sea salt, freshly ground black pepper and a pinch of paprika, to taste

sunflower oil for frying or coating the burgers

Chop the salmon finely or pulse 4 or 5 times in a food processor. Break up the goats' cheese with a fork and add it to the salmon, along with the chopped spring onions and SunBlush® tomatoes. Mix well or pulse again, but keep some texture – you don't want to reduce the mixture to a paste.

Finely chop the basil and add to the mixture, along with the breadcrumbs. Season with salt, pepper and a pinch of paprika, mix again and set the mixture aside for half an hour for the breadcrumbs to soften and absorb the moisture.

Divide the mixture and pat out into 6 burgers. Fry in a little oil, or rub both sides with oil and barbecue over an indirect heat, for about 6–7 minutes, turning once or twice during the cooking process. I quite like them on their own with salad and a salsa, but you could put them in a bap or bun with lime-flavoured mayo, sliced cucumber and shredded lettuce.

* I prefer to use the chilled SunBlush® tomatoes, which are sweeter and less pungent than the traditional sun-dried Italian ones in jars.

Best beer match Blonde, golden and amber ales, and lagers pair well with these burgers.

Thai tuna burgers with lime & coriander

serves 3–6

450g skinless, boneless tuna cut into chunks

80g quark

4 spring onions, trimmed and finely chopped

1 tsp finely grated garlic or garlic paste

1 tsp finely grated fresh ginger or ginger paste

grated rind of 1 small, unwaxed lime

2 tsp lime juice

2 tsp light soy sauce

1 tsp Thai fish sauce (nam pla)

a good shake of chilli sauce

40g natural dried breadcrumbs

3 tbsp finely chopped fresh coriander leaves

sunflower oil for frying or coating the burgers

Follow the method for the salmon recipe above. Serve with an Asian-style salad.

Best beer match Witbier or weissbier.

Pickled & smoked fish

Where wines struggle with pickled fish – and even some smoked fish preparations – beer triumphs, and Pilsener and Kölsch really come into their own.

Bistro blinis   Home-made blinis always look really great and they are not at all difficult to make. For a change, I like to have them with a smoked mackerel topping, but you could equally well use the more conventional smoked salmon. But, of course, there's nothing stopping you from having both.

serves 6 as a snack, 4 as a main meal

for the pancakes:

75g plain flour

75g buckwheat or wholemeal flour

1 level tbsp poppy seeds (optional but nice)

1 level tsp baking powder

½ level tsp fine sea salt

2 large free-range eggs

200ml full cream milk

25g melted butter + 25g butter for
  greasing the pan

for the dill cream:

1 x 142ml carton soured cream

1 x 150g carton unsweetened Greek yoghurt

2 tbsp finely chopped fresh dill

sea salt, to taste

for the topping:

3 medium-sized peppered mackerel fillets, skinned
  and flaked

1 medium-sized red onion, very finely chopped

2 lemons, cut into 4 wedges

To make the pancakes mix the dry ingredients in a bowl, leaving a hollow in the centre. Separate the eggs and mix the yolks with the milk and 25g of melted butter and gradually pour into the flour, stirring continually. Just before cooking, beat the egg whites until soft and fold into the pancake mixture.

Mix the soured cream with the yoghurt. Add 2 tbsp of the finely chopped onion, dill, salt to taste and mix together well.

Heat a pancake pan or non-stick frying pan over a medium heat, add a small knob of butter, swirl round the pan and wipe of the excess with a couple of sheets of kitchen towel. Put 4 tbsp of the pancake mix in the pan, then, when bubbles begin to appear on the surface (about 45 seconds), flip them over with a palette knife and cook the other side. Place on a warm plate covered with a clean tea towel while you make the remaining pancakes, greasing the pan with a little butter between each batch.

Serve each blini topped with a few flakes of smoked mackerel, a dollop of dill cream and a little chopped onion.

* You could also top some of the blinis with smoked salmon, soured cream and a little lumpfish roe.

Best beer match Perfect with a Pilsener.

Sweet & sour herring, beetroot & potato salad

If you're not already a herring convert, this should convince you.

serves 4 as a starter or as part of a smorgasbord

500g tub Scottish rollmop herrings

250g freshly cooked new potatoes, cooled
  and diced

1 large sweet–sour cucumber, diced

2 rounded tbsp soured cream

2 fresh cooked (not pickled) beetroot
  (about 75–100g), cubed

1 heaped tbsp finely chopped fresh dill

freshly ground black pepper

Drain the herrings, reserving the onions, pickle and
juice. Unroll the herrings, cut in half lengthways and cut
each piece into four. Put into a shallow dish with the
diced potatoes, half the reserved onion from the rollmop
herrings, any pickled cucumber and the diced cucumber.
  Mix the soured cream with 4 tbsp of the reserved
marinade from the rollmop herrings. Just before serving
pour over the soured cream mixture, add the beetroot,
season with freshly ground black pepper and mix
together lightly. Sprinkle with dill. Serve with a cucumber
and herb salad and rye bread.

Best beer match A light lager or a Pilsener.

Smoked fish pie

A good fish pie is hard to beat, and the addition of smoked fish makes it particularly beer-friendly.

serves 4–5

300g naturally smoked (i.e. undyed) cod or haddock
  fillets (or, even better, the flesh from an Arbroath smokie)
300g fresh cod or haddock fillets
1 slice of onion
1 bay leaf
a few peppercorns
600ml semi-skimmed milk
40g butter
40g plain flour
200g tomatoes, skinned, de-seeded and diced
3 level tbsp freshly grated Parmesan cheese
sea salt and freshly ground black pepper, to taste

for the potato topping:

750g boiling potatoes, peeled and quartered
15g butter
50–60ml warm milk
2 tbsp freshly grated Parmesan cheese
sea salt and freshly ground white or black pepper, to taste

Cut the fillets into pieces that will fit into a medium to large saucepan and lay them in the pan skin-side up. Add the onion, bay leaf and peppercorns, and pour over enough milk to cover. Bring slowly to the boil, then turn the heat right down and simmer for 4–5 minutes. Remove the fish with a fish slice and strain the milk into a measuring jug.

Melt the butter in a non-stick saucepan, stir in the flour and cook for a few seconds. Take the pan off the heat and tip about 2/3 of the strained milk into the flour, whisking continually. Bring to the boil, turn the heat down and leave to simmer, adding a little extra milk if it seems too thick. Season with pepper and a little salt.

Remove the skin from the fish and flake it, carefully removing any bones. Tip the fish and tomatoes into the sauce and stir in the Parmesan. Check the seasoning, adding extra salt and pepper to taste, and tip into a shallow pie dish or baking dish.

While you're assembling the pie, put the potatoes in a saucepan, cover with cold water and bring to the boil. Cook for about 20 minutes until you can stick the point of a knife in them easily. Drain the potatoes, return them to the pan and cut them up roughly with a knife. Mash them thoroughly with a potato masher or fork. Beat in the butter and warm milk. Season with salt and pepper.

Spread the potato evenly over the top of the fish, roughing up the surface with the prongs of a fork, and sprinkle with the remaining Parmesan. Place the pie on a baking tray under a preheated grill and grill for 5–10 minutes until the potato is nicely browned.

* You can assemble the pie ahead of time, refrigerate it, then bake it in a hot oven (200°C/400°F/Gas 6) for about 35–40 minutes.

Best beer match You could go two ways with this: a traditional British bitter (we enjoyed Harveys Sussex Best Bitter with it) or a stout (Mackeson's proved a good match).

Fishy tales

It's lunchtime at Gitte Kik, a traditional smørrebrød restaurant in Copenhagen, and I'm gazing in complete amazement at the plates of herring before me – there must be a choice of at least six different cures. I take just one back to the table. A chilled glass of lager arrives with a frozen aquavit chaser. 'The herring has to swim,' jokes my new-found friend, Henrik.

The match is perfect, the freshness and bitterness of the lager and aromatic spirit picking up on the dill-flavoured cure, cutting through the oiliness of the fish. It also works brilliantly with home-cured gravlax and delicately smoked eel. Why don't we eat dishes like this more often? You can find Mediterranean dishes like spaghetti alla vongole and salade Niçoise all over the world, so why not the seafood dishes of northern and central Europe? And they're just great with beer.

Other memories: Swedish crayfish cooked with lager and dill – sweet, lobster-like meat, fresh beer, what's not to like? A recent Polish dinner, organized by Slow Food Krakow. Some really strong oily smoky herring and salmon that assaults the palate with all the force of a chargrilled steak. There's tricky-to-match fresh horseradish and a beetroot and cranberry relish, too. Polish lager to the rescue.

On to Germany with its unfashionable river fish – pike and carp. There's a slight earthiness in the taste that really needs a fresh-tasting Pilsener. Further south, in Munich, we wander round the Oktoberfest. There's a wonderful smell of grilling, whole fish speared on stakes, lined up like the chorus in a Busby Berkeley musical. The fish is wrapped in paper, as it would be at a chippy. We perch our bundles precariously on the ledge at the back of the smoke pits and dig out the chunks of crisp smoky flesh, washing it down with a light helles beer.

On the back streets of Brussels, plates of salmon in a creamy sauce and my first taste of draught gueuze. At first it seems as mouth-puckeringly sour as a pickled lime but then I see where it's taking me, cutting through the rich fish and cream. Later, in the Belga Queen, one of Belgium's trendiest beer restaurants, we find it goes equally well with eel and green sauce. What would that do to wine? Doesn't bear thinking about.

Back in Blighty. We're sitting in a pub garden, the umbrella shading us from the scorching midday sun. Two plates of crisply battered fish and chips arrive, followed by two pints of the landlord's best bitter, perfectly served, cellar cool. Anyone who thinks beer doesn't go with fish needs their head examined…

" When people in this country think of beer and fish, they only really think of using beer for making batter or drinking cans of it when they go fishing. But we've been eating fish on this island for much longer than most of us have been drinking wine, and what did we drink with fish originally? Beer. People around the world have been drinking beer with fish – not just in the countries mentioned above, but also in the States, Australia, even China. Matching it just requires a little bit of creativity. "

Fish & chips

If you've never tried making home-made fish and chips, give it a go – the flavour and texture are so much better than you'll find at the average chippy. A deep-fat fryer will make the job a lot easier.

serves 2

vegetable or corn oil for frying

2 x 175g even-sized boneless, skinless cod or
  haddock fillets

for the batter:

55g self-raising flour + a little extra for coating the fish

¼ tsp sea salt

1 tbsp sunflower oil

75ml chilled lager or other light beer

1 small egg white

for the chips:

400g Maris Piper or other chipping potatoes

for the tartare sauce:

2 heaped tbsp French-style mayonnaise

1 tsp capers, rinsed and finely chopped

2 gherkins, finely chopped

1 tbsp finely chopped parsley (optional)

" The beauty of fish and chips is that I don't know a single person who doesn't like it, and you can make the batter with pretty much any beer that takes your fancy. Experiment with it and you'll find a personalized recipe that becomes a family classic for a lifetime. "

First peel and cut up the potatoes into even-sized chips. Put them in a saucepan of cold water, give them a good swirl and dry them with a clean tea towel. Make sure there is enough oil in the fryer to come up to the minimum level and heat to 150°C/300°F.

Make the batter by sifting the flour into a bowl with the salt. Make a dip in the centre, add the oil and 2/3 of the beer and gradually work in the flour with a wooden spoon. Add the remaining beer and beat until smooth.

Once the oil has reached the correct temperature, transfer the chips to the frying basket, lower into the oil and fry for 5 minutes without colouring. Remove from the pan and drain. Increase the frying temperature to 180°C/350°F.

Whip the egg white until stiff and fold into the batter. Dip the cod fillets into the flour and then into the batter and lower into the oil. Fry for about 4–5 minutes until the batter is crisp and golden. Remove with a slotted spoon and set aside in a warm place. Increase

the frying temperature to 190°C/375°F.

While the fish is cooking, mix the ingredients for the tartare sauce.

When the oil has reached the right temperature return the chips to the oil again and fry for another 2–3 minutes until crisp and brown. Serve with the fish, tartare sauce and a wedge of lemon. Peas – mushy or otherwise – are strongly recommended.

Best beer match Good British bitter like Coniston Bluebird or any good full-flavoured British ale about 4–5.5% ABV. Bitter is lighter and more refreshing; ale mimics the taste of malt vinegar.

chicken & other birds

'Beer and birds. Great combination. Blonde, brown...' Ahem, Will, we're talking about ales, not girls. But, yes, they do go well together. Especially roast chicken, as you'll see from the recipes in this chapter, not to mention the legendary beer-can chicken, possibly the best chicken recipe in the world.

Chicken is, of course, not the only bird in town. There's turkey, which is actually just like a big chicken, poussin (mini-chicken), quail (essentially a micro-chicken) and guineafowl, which has slightly more flavour than chicken. Basically, they're all meats you could have with the same beer that you'd have with a chicken prepared in a similar way.

You really only need to think differently when you start pondering matches for duck, goose and really gamey game like pheasant (see pages 80–1).

Chicken is, however, a chameleon-like ingredient that picks up any flavour you put with it. With most recipes, it's more important how you cook the bird than the fact that it's chicken. (This applies to the other birds just mentioned, too.) Just take a look at these different chicken dishes and the beers that you might drink with them:

* Chicken pot pie (chicken in a creamy sauce) – goes well with smooth, sweet golden and blonde ales.

* Jerk chicken – the spiciness and the likelihood of an accompanying barbecue sauce suggests a more full-flavoured beer, such as a Viennese amber lager or an American IPA.

* Southern fried chicken – the fact that it's fried counts for more than the fact that it's chicken. A light Pilsener or English bitter would be a good pairing.

* Thai green chicken curry – again, it's the accompanying flavours you have to focus on: lime, coriander, chilli and coconut. A light wheat beer, like a witbier or bière blanche, would be the best option.

Get the point?

In praise of roast chicken

No matter how many different chicken recipes you try, you always come back to roast chicken, the perfect comfort meal. Everyone has their own favourite recipe, whether it's Jamie Oliver's or their Mum's: the common factor should be moist, succulent meat and irresistibly savoury, crispy skin.

There are two recipes for roast chicken in this chapter that we're sure you will enjoy. One is the classic Oktoberfest chicken (see below), slathered with butter. The other, given on pages 72–3, is the great American institution Beer-can chicken. Once you've made it, you'll never think of barbecuing birds in any other way. And if you can't bear to abandon Mum's recipe? Well, at least try the recipe opposite for delicious creamy beer gravy – much better, by far, than Bisto…

Oktoberfest chicken

This recipe, which I've edited slightly from the version in the *Oktoberfest Insider Guide* by Sabine Kafer, comes from Andreas Geitl, chef at Winzerer Fahndl. The secret is the lavish last-minute slathering with butter.

serves 2

1 small chicken (about 1.2kg) – Geitl stresses the importance of the bird being dry-plucked
sea salt and freshly ground black pepper
a good handful of fresh parsley with their stalks
50g unsalted butter

An hour before roasting, season the chicken generously with pepper and salt 'so that even the preparation makes your mouth water'.

Wash the parsley, shake dry, chop roughly and stuff inside the chicken. If you have a rotisserie attachment in your oven, preheat the oven to 220°C/425°F/Gas 7, skewer the chicken on the spit and roast for about an hour. Alternatively, preheat the oven to 200°C/400°F/Gas 6, and put the bird breast-side downwards in a roasting tin. (Geitl recommends not using a fan oven or fan oven setting for this, as it will dry the meat out – not sure I agree with that.)

Roast for about 30 minutes, then turn the bird breast-side upwards and finish cooking (allow 25 minutes per 450g in total – it should take just over an hour for a bird of this size.)

Either way – and this is crucial – 15 minutes before the end of the cooking time, coat the bird with fresh, soft but not runny butter. Repeat 4–5 times.

To check if the chicken is ready, stick a skewer or the point of a sharp knife into the thickest part of the leg. The juices should run clear. Cut the chicken in half down the breastbone and serve half a portion each.

Best beer match At the Oktoberfest in Munich, this dish would be served with a light helles beer but we prefer it with a classic Oktoberfest Märzen (see opposite) or a golden lager like Budweiser Budvar.

Light blonde gravy for chicken

serves 4

1 tbsp plain flour

250ml home-made chicken stock or stock made with
  ½ an organic chicken stock cube

75–100ml blonde ale

1 tbsp double cream

a squeeze of lemon or a few drops of cider vinegar
  (optional – see method)

a little malt extract or soft butter (optional – see method)

sea salt and freshly ground black pepper, to taste

At the end of the roasting period, remove the chicken from the roasting tin and transfer to a carving dish. Pour off all except 1 tbsp of pan juices. Add the plain flour and stir into the juices, then slowly add the chicken stock, working any nice stuck-on caramelized juices off the side and bottom of the tin.

Add 75ml of the beer and slowly bring the gravy to just below boiling point, stirring it from time to time. Add the cream, turn the heat down and simmer for a couple of minutes. Adjust the seasoning, adding salt and pepper to taste, a squeeze of lemon or a few drops of cider vinegar if it needs sharpening, and a little malt extract or butter if it seems too bitter (see Gravy tips on page 98).

Strain and pour into a warm jug.

* If you want to make this gravy for grilled chicken, cook a chopped onion in a little oil and butter until golden, then add the flour and proceed as above.

" The main type of beer drunk at the Oktoberfest is light helles lager served in huge foaming steins (tankards). It's not a great brew by any means but it hits the spot. Beers labelled 'Oktoberfest' are more commonly Märzen beers, so-called because they are brewed in March but aren't released until September. They're strong golden lagers (5–6% ABV) with a sweet malt character. "

Beer-can chicken

I can't remember where I first read about beer-can chicken but it changed my life. It has to be the best-ever way of cooking a bird – a cross between roasting and barbecuing. The whole process is so quick and the result so tasty, you just wouldn't believe it. It also looks quite hilariously comic. Basically, what you're doing is forcing beer-flavoured steam up inside the chicken while the fat from the skin runs down the body, constantly basting it and giving it a super-crisp, spicy skin.

In terms of detailed guidance, I rely on the seminal *Beer-Can Chicken* by Steven Raichlen, America's barbecue king. After you've cooked the recipe below once or twice, you will almost certainly want to buy the book. You may also want to change your barbecue to one with a larger-domed lid so that you can fit in two or more chickens – a necessary extravagance once you get the beer-can chicken (BCC) habit.

serves 4

1 small to medium-sized chicken – about
  1.3–1.5kg
about 1 tbsp jerk seasoning or other rub
330ml can of lager
a little sunflower or vegetable oil
You will need a barbecue with a large-domed lid

Rinse the chicken inside and out and dry thoroughly with kitchen towel. Remove any surplus fat from the carcass and sprinkle the inside with about 1 tsp of the seasoning, rubbing it in well. Sprinkle the rest of the seasoning over the chicken and rub it in. Leave to marinate for half an hour or so. Fire up the barbecue.

Pour half the contents of the beer can into a glass. Smear the can lightly with the sunflower or vegetable oil, and lower the chicken onto the can so that it stands upright, propped up by its legs. Set the can and chicken on the barbecue rack, cover with the lid, and cook over an indirect heat for about 50 minutes

to an hour, until the juices run clear when you pierce the leg with a skewer.

Holding the can with a pair of tongs, very carefully remove the chicken from the can and set aside on a carving tray. Rest for 5–10 minutes, then carve the chicken and serve with a barbecue sauce or a salsa.

BCC barbecue sauce

2 tbsp sunflower oil
1 small onion, peeled and finely chopped
1 clove of garlic, peeled and crushed
1 tsp of the seasoning rub used for the chicken
1 tbsp soft brown sugar
4 tbsp tomato ketchup
2–3 tbsp cider vinegar
1–2 tsp Worcestershire sauce
juice of ½ an orange
150–175ml Leffe Brune or other brown beer

Heat the oil in a small saucepan, add the onion and cook for about 5–6 minutes until they begin to soften.

Add the crushed garlic and jerk seasoning, cook for a minute then stir in the sugar. Add the tomato ketchup, 2 tbsp of the cider vinegar, Worcestershire sauce and orange juice. Stir, then pour in half the beer. Bring to the boil, turn the heat down and simmer for about half an hour, adding more beer, as needed, if it gets too thick. Sieve and serve.

Best beer match An amber lager or ale, or an American IPA.

Other pointers & tips

* Type of chicken: the beauty about BCC is that you can use an ordinary chicken and it will taste great – not that I'm recommending an intensively reared one but any humanely reared free-range bird will do.

* Type of rub: you will want something with a bit of a kick (this is a barbecue, after all), so go for a jerk or Cajun-type spice mix. (Seasoned Pioneers and Fiddes Payne are two good suppliers.) Barbecue aficionados make their own rubs, but I haven't yet come up with a better blend than the ready-made ones. And, hell, they save time.

* Type of beer: obviously, it has to be a beer in a can, which limits your options. But there's no reason why you shouldn't dispose of the contents of the can and pour in a beer of your choice. (Canned stout has an interesting effect, making the chicken taste maltier and smokier.)

* Number of chickens and cans: if you're cooking for 4–6 people, it's better to barbecue two smaller chickens than one bigger one – it's easier to control and there's more crispy skin. But if you're making BCC for a crowd of people, you can use bigger birds and 660ml cans of beer.

* Amount of beer: don't forget to pour away (or drink) half the contents of the beer before you insert it in the chicken, otherwise it will cascade out of the can and onto the coals.

* Oiling the can: smear the can with a little sunflower or vegetable oil so that you can easily slip the chicken onto it and, more importantly, remove it safely at the end of the cooking period. An oven glove and a pair of tongs will also help you to do this safely.

Sierra Nevada chicken

A Belgian-style chicken stew made with a classic American ale – chicken casserole re-invented.

serves 4

3 tbsp sunflower oil or light olive oil

125g smoked bacon lardons

500g skinless, boneless chicken thighs cut into
  large chunks

1 medium onion, peeled and roughly chopped

1 large carrot, peeled and thinly sliced

2 sticks of celery, trimmed and thinly sliced

1 clove of garlic, peeled and crushed

½ tsp finely chopped fresh thyme or ¼ tsp dried thyme

1 level tbsp plain flour

300ml fresh chicken stock or stock made from ½ an
  organic chicken stock cube

150ml Sierra Nevada Pale Ale + a little extra to finish
  the dish

300g new potatoes

125g chestnut mushrooms, rinsed and sliced

a handful of roughly chopped flatleaf parsley

sea salt and freshly ground black pepper, to taste

Heat 2 tbsp of oil in a large frying pan and brown the lardons lightly (about 3–4 minutes). Remove to a casserole with a slotted spoon, then lightly brown the chicken pieces. Transfer them to the casserole with the bacon, turn down the heat in the frying pan and add the chopped onion. Cook until starting to soften (about 3–4 minutes), then add the sliced carrot and celery, stir and cook for a couple of minutes more.

Tip the vegetables into the casserole, stir, cover with a lid and leave to cook for 10 minutes over a very low heat for the flavours to amalgamate. Remove the lid, add the crushed garlic and thyme, cook for a few seconds, then stir in the flour and cook for a minute. Add the chicken stock and Sierra Nevada pale ale, and bring up to boiling point. Turn the heat right down, re-cover the pan and simmer for 20 minutes.

Cut the new potatoes into even-sized chunks, add them to the casserole, stir well and continue to simmer until the potatoes are cooked (another 15–20 minutes), adding the sliced mushrooms about 10 minutes before the end of the cooking time.

Splash in a little extra Sierra Nevada Pale Ale (about 2 tbsp), season with salt and pepper, and cook for another 2–3 minutes. Stir in the chopped parsley and serve the stew in large shallow soup bowls.

Best beer match Sierra Nevada Pale Ale or a Belgian-style blonde ale like Leffe.

Chicken Caesar salad

We love this hearty version of Caesar salad. Both the chicken and the Parmesan make it a great beer match.

serves 2–3

2 tbsp sunflower oil or light olive oil

1 tbsp lemon juice

a pinch of dried oregano

1 large or two smaller skinless, boneless chicken breasts, cut into strips

1 cos (romaine) lettuce or 2–3 Little Gem lettuces

50g home-made or shop-bought croutons (broken up bruschetta bases taste better than croutons in packs)

a few chives

40g shaved Parmesan cheese

for the dressing:

1 large clove of garlic, peeled and chopped

2–3 anchovy fillets, roughly chopped

1 tsp Dijon mustard

1 medium egg yolk (optional)

3–4 tbsp light olive oil

1 tbsp double cream or crème fraîche

freshly squeezed lemon juice, to taste

freshly ground black pepper, to taste

Mix together the oil, lemon juice and oregano, and marinate the chicken strips for 30 minutes to an hour. Heat a ridged grill or heavy-duty frying pan for 2–3 minutes, shake the marinade off the chicken strips, then cook them briefly on all sides until lightly browned (about 2–3 minutes). Set aside to cool.

Pull the leaves off the lettuce(s), discarding any damaged leaves, and plunge them into a sink or bowl full of iced water. Leave for 10–15 minutes to crisp, then shake off the excess water and dry in a salad spinner or with a tea towel.

To make the dressing, pound the garlic and anchovies together with a mortar and pestle until they form a paste. Add the mustard and egg yolk, if using, the oil as if you were making a mayonnaise. Stir in the crème fraîche, then season to taste with lemon juice and freshly ground black pepper. (You shouldn't need any salt.) Add a splash of warm water if the dressing is too thick. (Alternatively, make the dressing in a food processor.)

Break the bruschetta bases into rough chunks and cut the chives into three. Arrange the lettuce leaves in a shallow salad bowl and scatter over the chicken pieces and croutons. Spoon or pour over the dressing, and scatter the Parmesan shavings and chives over the top.

Best beer match A blonde or golden ale, such as Duvel or Schiehallion, hits the spot here.

Smoked duck salad with raspberry beer dressing

Fruit beers like kriek and frambozen pair particularly well with duck, which is logical when you think how well cherries and raspberries go with duck in the kitchen. Here, I've used a raspberry beer to make a tart fruity dressing, adding pomegranate seeds and sun-dried berries for colour and extra fruity flavour.

serves 4 as a starter, 2 as a main course

a small pack of mixed salad leaves

100g pecan nuts

200g thinly sliced smoked duck breast

½ a pomegranate and/or 50–100g sun-dried berries

for the dressing:

1 level tsp clear honey

75ml raspberry beer

75ml grapeseed oil

sea salt, freshly ground black pepper and a pinch of
   dry mustard, to taste

First, make the dressing. Whisk together the honey and raspberry beer, then gradually whisk in the oil.

Season to taste with salt, pepper and a pinch of mustard and whisk again. Scoop the seeds out of the pomegranate and pick out the pith. Pour off any juice into the dressing.

Divide the salad leaves between the plates, scatter over the pecans and drape the duck slices artistically over the top. Spoon over the dressing and scatter over the pomegranate seeds and/or sun-dried berries (using the smaller quantity if you're using the seeds as well).

Best beer match Serve the same beer you use for the dressing.

Duck & Kwak

Lousy pun, we know, but we couldn't resist it. And, fortunately, the match is a great one. The duck is given an oriental twist with a soy and honey glaze.

serves 4

1 medium-sized Gressingham or other premium-quality duck (about 2kg)

2 tbsp clear honey

2 tbsp light soy sauce + a little extra for the sauce

2¼ tbsp hoisin sauce

125ml hot beef stock or stock made with 1 tsp Marmite or Bovril

2 tbsp Kwak

sea salt and freshly ground black pepper, to taste

Remove any excess fat from the inside of the carcass and prick the skin with the point of a sharp knife or fork. Pour a kettle of boiling water slowly over the skin, turning the duck halfway through. Pat dry and leave lightly covered for an hour.

Heat the oven to 220°C/425°F/Gas 7. Season the duck with salt and freshly ground black pepper, rubbing it into the skin. Roast for 30 minutes, then pour off the fat into the tin. Turn the heat down to 190°C/375°F/Gas 5 and cook for a further 30 minutes.

Mix the honey and soy sauce with a few drops of hoisin sauce. Remove the duck from the oven, pour off the fat again and brush the honey and soy mixture over the skin. Return to the oven, cook for another 10 minutes, then brush the marinade over again. Repeat once more after another 10 minutes' cooking.

Remove the duck from the oven and rest in a warm place for 10–15 minutes. Put the remaining hoisin sauce in a bowl and gradually stir in the stock and Kwak. Season with a few drops of soy sauce. Pour the fat out of the roasting pan and pour in the sauce.

Bring to the boil, scraping off any burnt-on juices, then adjust the seasoning to taste.

Carve the duck and serve with roast or sautéed potatoes and some stir-fried broccoli or greens. It would also go well with soba noodles.

Best beer match Kwak, obviously, but other strong Belgian ales, particularly dark abbey and Trappist beers, would also work, as would a dark French bière de garde.

❝ Kwak is named after the fantastically monikered Pauwel Kwak, who first brewed it in 1791. The beer is best known for the glass in which it is traditionally served. Shaped like a yard of ale and stored hanging in a wooden frame, the glass, according to legend, was made for coachmen needing a way to enjoy beer while still on the coach (Napoleonic Code forbade them leaving the coach and sharing a drink with the passengers). Kwak developed the glass so that the coachmen could hang it on the coach and have it conveniently to hand. ❞

Pot roast pheasant with bacon, onion & apple & spiced juniper cabbage

Pot-roasting pheasant is a great way to tenderize it. You can also make this with guineafowl or partridge.

serves 4

2 tbsp olive oil

2 oven-ready pheasants

100g bacon lardons

1 medium to large onion, peeled and sliced

1 medium to large apple, peeled and sliced

20g butter

1 large clove of garlic, peeled and finely chopped

2 tsp fresh thyme or 1 tsp dried thyme

250–300ml chicken or vegetable stock

sea salt and freshly ground black pepper, to taste

Heat the oil in a large deep cast iron casserole and brown the birds lightly on all sides. Remove from the pot and set aside.

Fry the lardons until the fat starts to run, then add the onions and apple, stir and cook for 2–3 minutes. Add the butter, garlic and thyme and cook for another 2 minutes or so, then pour in half the stock.

Return the pheasants to the pan breast-side down, and spoon over the sauce. Put a lid on the pan and cook over a low heat for about 1¼ hours, turning the pheasants every so often and adding more stock as needed.

Once the pheasants are cooked, set them aside and skim any surface fat off the juices. Add any remaining stock and adjust the seasoning. Serve with the spiced juniper cabbage and celeriac mash or a parsnip purée.

Spiced juniper cabbage

10 juniper berries

½ tsp cumin seeds

¾ tsp coarse sea salt

½ tsp black peppercorns

3 tbsp olive oil

½ a Savoy or other green cabbage, finely shredded

3 tbsp vegetable stock or water

Grind the seasoning with a mortar and pestle. Heat the oil in a casserole or saucepan and tip in the cabbage, turning it so that all the leaves are coated with oil. Put a lid on the pan and cook over a low heat for 5 minutes until the leaves have partially collapsed.

Stir in the ground spices and mix well, add 2 tbsp of stock, replace the lid and continue to cook on a very low heat for about 25 minutes, adding more stock, as necessary. Check the seasoning, adding more salt and pepper, if required.

Beer match Perfect for an oude gueuze or a Belgian red ale like Rodenbach.

" Gueuze, pronounced ('jerss' or 'jersser' in Flemish), is a bit of an acquired taste – like olives or espresso coffee. The first time I tried it, I found it really quite unpleasantly sour and bitter, but I'm gradually coming round. Mum loves it but then she's into extreme tastes. Anyway, what you need to know is that it's a blend of young and old lambic (wild-yeasted) beers, it's given a second fermentation in the bottle and it has considerable ageing potential. Matured gueuze is referred to as oude (pronounced 'owder') gueuze. "

meat feasts

Meat is regarded as natural red wine territory but no beer lover needs persuading that ale is every bit as good an accompaniment. This is especially true of classic British meat dishes such as roasts and pies, where beer's natural affinity with pastry and potatoes reinforces the match. Beer can also be used to brilliant effect as a flavouring ingredient in such classics as steak pie and cottage pie.

* A good British ale makes a wonderfully robust stew (with or without dumplings) or flavoursome gravy to accompany a slap-up Sunday roast or a comforting plate of sausage and mash.

* The sweet, fruity flavours of blonde and amber ales and lagers are great with pork, their carbonation cutting through the slight fattiness of cuts such as pork belly or shoulder. They also go well with fruit accompaniments like apple, and sweet vegetables like butternut squash.

* A strong Belgian red ale, like Rodenbach, can be a marvellous accompaniment for roast or braised lamb, just as it is for feathered game. Or serve rosy pink lamb cutlets with a raspberry or cherry beer, just as you'd serve it with a fruity sauce or relish.

* Dark porters and stouts work well with stews but they can also provide an effective contrast to boiled or baked ham or gammon in a similar way as they do to seafood (see my twist on the American classic Ham and Coke on page 99).

* Beer's also a natural for barbecues and grilled meats. Powerful red wines can sometimes create a palate overload with the kaleidoscope of flavours from the various relishes and salads that typically accompany a barbecue, but clean thirst-quenching lagers and ales provide welcome refreshment. Or try a smoky Rauchbier or other smoked beer – sensational with some sweet, sticky glazed ribs.

* Beer can also be used as a marinade or glaze to boost the flavour and intensity of meats that need only a short cooking time. Beer does not have that sometimes over-sharp acidity that wine has, which can change the flavour of the meat.

* Warming, seasonal winter beers are the most natural thing to drink with meaty winter dishes. They also make perfect stews and casseroles.

In fact, the only thing beer isn't so great with is sauces made with wine... But how many of you are using wine in the kitchen anyway?

Roast pork belly with black pudding & potato & apple purée

Pork is my favourite roast with beer, especially if it has loads of crackling as a joint of pork belly does. (This cut is well worth ordering from a good butcher or organic meat supplier.) The apple and potato purée is a German dish called, appropriately, Himmel und Erde (heaven and earth) and is the perfect accompaniment.

serves 4–6

1 tsp coarse sea salt
1 tsp black peppercorns
2 tsp coriander seeds
1 large clove of garlic, peeled and chopped
2 tbsp sunflower or light olive oil
1.35kg pork belly in a single piece on the bone
500ml chicken stock
sea salt and freshly ground black pepper, to taste
250g black pudding, skinned and sliced

Preheat the oven to 230°C/450°F/Gas 8.

Put the coarse sea salt, peppercorns and coriander seeds in a mortar, and pound with a pestle until coarsely ground. Add the chopped garlic and pound again, then add 1 tbsp of oil to create a thick paste.

With a sharp knife cut into the pork flesh either side so you can push the spice mixture into the meat and rub it over the flesh and into the cuts you've made (but not over the skin). Put the joint on a wire rack over a roasting tin and add a splash of the stock to the pan to stop the spices from burning and roast for 20 minutes.

Turn the heat down to 180°C/350°F/Gas 4 and cook for another hour and 40 minutes, pouring off the fat halfway through and adding a little extra liquid to the tin if the juices threaten to burn. (Don't baste it though – you'll spoil the crackling!) Transfer the joint to another roasting tin, turn the heat back up to 230°C/450°F/Gas 8 and continue cooking until the crackling is good and crisp. Set aside and rest for 10 minutes (but don't cover or the steam will make the crackling soft).

Carefully pour any accumulated fat off the first roasting tin, pour in half the remaining stock and work round the tin with a wooden spoon to incorporate all the caramelized meat juices. Add more stock, if needed, to get a thin but tasty gravy, and season with salt and freshly ground black pepper.

Heat the remaining oil in another pan and fry the black pudding slices on both sides until crisp. Carve the meat into chunks and serve with the black pudding, potato and apple purée and some lightly cooked, buttered Brussels tops or cabbage.

Potato & apple purée

600g boiling potatoes
500g Bramley apples or other sharp cooking apples
sea salt and freshly ground black pepper, to taste

Cut the potatoes into even-sized pieces, cover with cold water, bring to the boil and cook until tender (about 18–20 minutes).

Peel, core and slice the apples and put in a saucepan with 2 tbsp of water. Cover and cook on a low heat, stirring occasionally until the apples are soft and fluffy. Beat well with a wooden spoon.

Drain and mash the potatoes, then add the apple purée and beat well. Season to taste with salt and freshly ground black pepper.

Best beer match Plenty of possibilities: a Märzen Oktoberfest beer, a Belgian or Northern French blonde, an American IPA, a Viennese-style lager or a double bock like Schneider Aventinus.

Steaks & chops

Given that Will runs an American-style steakhouse, Hawksmoor, we've spent a fair bit of time testing the combination of steak and American craft beer – purely in the interests of research, of course – and have to report that it's a great match. (We can particularly recommend the 600g bone-in sirloin with a Sierra Nevada Pale Ale.)

Unfortunately, at home most of us don't have access to quite the same quality of meat or the same expertise at handling charcoal grills, so I've devised a recipe that makes ordinary steak taste quite special. Note that you don't need to marinade it for more than an hour.

Steak with Innis & Gunn
Innis & Gunn is a full-flavoured ale that is aged in whisky barrels, which makes it as good a partner for steak as red wine.

serves 2

2 x 250g thick sirloin steaks, well trimmed

1 medium onion, peeled, halved and thinly sliced

200ml Innis & Gunn or other full-bodied ale

2 small bay leaves

6–7 peppercorns

2 tbsp sunflower or other light cooking oil

10g butter

1 tsp plain flour

1 tsp tomato ketchup

sea salt, freshly ground black pepper and sugar, to taste

a dash of full-flavoured whisky, such as Monkey's Shoulder

Trim any excess fat and sinew off the steaks. Put a few onion slices in the bottom of a shallow dish and place the steaks on top. Pour over the Innis & Gunn, add a couple more onion slices, saving the rest for the sauce. Add the bay leaves and peppercorns, cover and leave to marinate for an hour, turning the steaks halfway through.

Remove the steaks from the marinade and pat dry, and rub a little oil onto each side. Heat a frying pan until hot (about 2 minutes), then place the steaks in the pan. Cook for 2–3 minutes, then turn the steaks over and cook for 1–3 minutes the other side, depending on how well done you want them.

Set the steaks aside on a plate and cover lightly. Add 1 tbsp of oil to the pan, then add the butter. Fry the remaining onion in the pan for a couple of minutes until beginning to brown. Turn the heat down a little and stir in the flour.

Strain the marinade into the pan and stir until thick. Add the tomato ketchup and a splash of whisky (about 1 tbsp) and cook for another minute. Add a little boiling water if the sauce is too thick, then season to taste with salt, freshly ground black pepper and a pinch of sugar, if you think the sauce needs it. Serve with chips or baked potatoes.

Best beer match Innis & Gunn or a strong dark Trappist ale.

Fat pork chops with Duvel & mushrooms

Beer can also be used to make a quick sauce for pan-fried meat, as in this splendidly robust dish. Note that I don't use the beer to deglaze the pan, which would accentuate its bitterness.

serves 2

2 fat pork loin chops, preferably organic

2 tbsp olive oil

25g butter

175g button mushrooms, wiped and thickly sliced

3 tbsp chicken or vegetable stock

75g Duvel or other strong Belgian-style ale

2 rounded tbsp crème fraîche

1 tsp Dijon mustard

1/2 tsp wine vinegar

sea salt and freshly ground black pepper, to taste

Pat the chops dry, cut through the fat at regular intervals to keep them flat in the pan, and season them with salt and pepper. Heat the pan for a couple of minutes. Add 1 tbsp of the oil and half the butter. When it stops foaming, lay the chops in the pan and brown for 3 minutes, then turn them over and brown the other side. Turn down the heat and continue to cook for another 10 minutes or so, turning them every few minutes.

Remove the chops from the pan and set them aside on a warm plate. Pour off the excess fat, add the remaining oil and butter, and sauté the mushrooms quickly until lightly browned, then transfer them to the plate with the chops.

Pour the stock into the pan, let it bubble up and sizzle, then turn the heat down and add the Duvel, working it round the pan to pick up any nice stuck-on crusty bits. When the beer has reduced by about a third, add the crème fraîche and mix thoroughly, then take off the heat and add the mustard and vinegar.

Put the chops and mushrooms in the pan and place over a very low heat, spooning the sauce over the chops. Heat through for about 5 minutes without boiling, check the seasoning, then serve. Good with some new potatoes and lightly cooked greens.

Best beer match Duvel would be the obvious choice but a darker Belgian ale would work, too.

Sticky barbecued ribs

You could use a proportion of beer in this sticky barbecue baste but, quite honestly, there's so much else going on there that you won't pick up that much flavour from it. Better to use the dish as a showcase for a really good porter or smoked beer.

serves 4–6

2kg pork spare ribs

for the basting sauce:

500g pack of creamed tomatoes

75g dark muscovado sugar

75ml cider vinegar

1 tbsp Worcestershire sauce

1 rounded tbsp mild chilli powder

a few drops (or more) of hot pepper sauce

2 tbsp bourbon or dark rum (optional but nice)

1 tbsp light olive or grapeseed oil + extra oil,
  if needed

2 large cloves of garlic

¼ tsp sea salt

Preheat the oven to 200°C/400°F/Gas 6.

Lay the ribs in a large tin or baking dish (or two smaller ones) and roast for 30 minutes.

Combine the basting sauce ingedients in a saucepan, bring to the boil, then simmer for 10 minutes. Check the seasoning, adding extra hot pepper sauce if you can take it. Drain the fat off the ribs and pour the basting sauce over them. Reduce the oven temperature to 190°C/375°F/Gas 5 and cook for a further hour to an hour and a quarter, basting the ribs regularly until the sauce has gone gooey and sticky and the ribs are well done. If they seem a bit dry, drizzle over a little more oil.

Serve with baked potatoes and a crunchy (preferably home-made) coleslaw.

Best beer match A great dish to drink with a good porter like Meantime London Porter or even a smoked beer like Rogue's Smoke Ale. If you want a lighter beer by way of contrast, try an amber ale or lager.

" You might think that combining barbecued food with smoked beer is a bit incendiary but, when the basting sauce is as sweet as this one, it works. The beers get their flavour from the malt being smoked over peat or wood such as beech or oak. The tradition is long-established in parts of Germany such as Franconia, in particular the town of Bamburg, and it has also been taken up by American producers such as the Alaskan Brewing Company and Rogue Brewery. "

Stews & braises

Braised meat and beer are natural bedfellows, producing wonderfully rich, cockle-warming stews and braises that are guaranteed to keep out the cold.

Shearers' stew
This is a great stew that they make at Will's gastropub, The Marquess, in north London. I love the crunchy toast topping.

serves 6

4–5 tbsp sunflower or vegetable oil

3 white onions, peeled and roughly chopped

a few sprigs of thyme

1.5kg lamb fillet or shoulder

3 tbsp plain flour, seasoned with salt and pepper

350ml lamb or beef stock

350ml strong ale

500g carrots, peeled or scrubbed and thickly
  sliced

sea salt and freshly ground black or white pepper, to taste

6 thick slices sourdough or similar country bread

Heat 3 tbsp of the oil in a large frying pan over a moderate heat, add the onions and thyme, and cook for about 10 minutes until soft, stirring occasionally.

Remove the onions from the pan with a slotted spoon and transfer to a casserole. Trim any excess (but not all) fat off the lamb, cut into cubes and toss in the seasoned flour. Add a little more oil to the frying pan and fry the lamb in batches until brown, adding it to the onions as you finish.

Deglaze the pan with 300ml of the stock and pour over the lamb and onions, then add the ale. Bring to the boil, stir, then simmer over a low heat for 1¹/₂ hours. Add the carrots and more stock if needed, then simmer for a further 30 minutes until the carrots are cooked. Season to taste with salt and pepper. Heat the oven to 220ºC/425ºF/Gas 7. Dip the bread slices in the sauce. Divide the remaining stew between individual pie dishes and top with a slice of the gravy-soaked bread. Bake each stew in the oven until the bread is nicely browned and crunchy.

Best beer match Any good, hearty British ale.

Carbonnade of beef with Orval

One of the striking things about cooking with beer is that you can afford to use your best bottles to cook with. This is based on a recipe in the splendid *Everyone Eats Well in Belgium Cookbook* by Ruth Van Waerebeek. Like most stews, it tastes even better if made a day ahead and reheated, which makes it a good dish to serve when you're having friends round.

serves 6

1.25kg leg of beef
3 tbsp plain flour, seasoned with sea salt and
  freshly ground black pepper
3–4 tbsp sunflower or vegetable oil
25g butter
450g onions, peeled and sliced
1 tsp finely chopped fresh thyme or a pinch
  of dried thyme
1 bay leaf
250ml beef stock
330ml Orval or other dark Trappist beer
1 tbsp demerara or brown sugar
1 tbsp cider vinegar
sea salt and freshly ground black pepper, to taste

Remove any excess fat and connective tissue from the meat, pat dry and cut into generous cubes. Put the flour in a shallow dish and season with salt and pepper.

Toss the meat in the flour, shaking off any excess. Heat 2 tbsp of oil in a large frying pan and fry the meat in batches until well browned, transferring it to a casserole as you finish each batch. Add extra oil if needed.

Once the meat is browned, melt the butter in the pan, add the onions, stir well and cook over a moderate heat until beginning to brown (about 10 minutes). Stir in the thyme and bay leaf, tip the onions onto the meat and stir well. Add the beef stock and Orval to the casserole, stir, bring to the boil, then half-cover the pan and simmer very slowly for about 2¹/₂ hours until the meat is completely tender.

Stir in the sugar and vinegar and cook for another 5 minutes. Season to taste with salt and black pepper, and serve with baked or boiled potatoes.

Best beer match Orval is the obvious choice but any dark Trappist ale would do.

" Trappist beers are abbey beers but not all abbey beers are Trappist. There are six Trappist breweries in Belgium (Chimay, Orval, Rochefort, Westmalle and Westveleteren) and one in Holland (Schaapskooi, which makes La Trappe). The description Trappist is more one of origin than style although – dark or light – they tend to be strong and richly flavoured. The terms dubbel and tripel are a more useful guide in that they flag up that the beer is one of the stronger brews the monastery makes. "

Steak & ale pie

A great gastropub classic that's equally rewarding to make and serve at home.

serves 6

1.25kg lean braising steak

2 tbsp plain flour, seasoned with sea salt and
 freshly ground black pepper

4–5 tbsp olive or sunflower oil

1 large onion, peeled and sliced

200ml fresh beef stock or stock made with
 ½ an organic beef stock cube

150ml Adnams Broadside or other full-bodied ale

1–2 tbsp tomato ketchup

1–2 tsp Worcestershire sauce

sea salt and freshly ground black pepper,
 to taste

a 375g pack frozen puff pastry, thawed

1 medium egg

Trim any excess fat off the steak, cut into generously sized cubes and dip them in the seasoned flour. Heat 3 tbsp of the oil in a frying pan and fry the cubed meat in batches until well browned, adding extra oil as necessary. Transfer each batch to a large casserole as you go.

Add a couple more tablespoons of oil to the pan and cook the onion slowly for about 10 minutes until soft. Stir in any leftover flour and cook for a minute. Add the stock and Broadside ale, working any caramelized juices off the side of the pan, then add the tomato ketchup and Worcestershire sauce. Bring to the boil and simmer for a couple of minutes.

Pour over the beef, stir and check the seasoning, adding salt, pepper and extra ketchup or Worcestershire sauce to taste, if needed. Cover and cook over a low heat for 2 hours or until tender, stirring occasionally. Transfer into a large pie dish and set aside until completely cold (2–3 hours).

Roll out the pastry quite thickly to fit the top of your pie dish, leaving some pastry over for the pie dish rim and for decoration. Cut long strips of pastry the width of the rim, dampen them with water and arrange round the rim of the dish. Dampen the top of the pastry rim, carefully lower the pastry lid into place, then cut off any overhanging edges. Crimp the edge of the pie and cut a slit in the centre of the pastry lid. Decorate the pie with pastry leaves, stars – whatever takes your fancy.

Just before baking, brush the pastry with beaten egg. Heat the oven to 220°C/425°F/Gas 7 and bake for 20 minutes, then turn the heat down to 190°C/375°F/Gas 5 and bake for 25–30 minutes more until the pastry is well browned and the juices are beginning to bubble under the pie crust.

Best beer match Any good full-bodied British ale such as Adnams Broadside or Bateman's XXXB.

Cottage pie with porter

You could also call this Landlord's pie if you want to make it sound more interesting. Adding porter to a cottage pie makes a fantastically rich, savoury filling.

serves 4

3 tbsp olive or sunflower oil

450g minced beef

1 medium to large onion, peeled and finely chopped

2 carrots (about 150g), peeled and finely chopped

½ tsp dried thyme

1 level tbsp plain flour

225ml beef stock or stock made with 1 level tsp
   Bovril or ½ beef stock cube

175ml London porter or stout

2–3 tsp Worcestershire sauce

1 tbsp tomato ketchup (optional)

sea salt and freshly ground black pepper, to taste

for the potato topping:

800g boiling potatoes, peeled and quartered

25g butter

50–75ml warm milk

sea salt and freshly ground black pepper, to taste

Heat a large frying pan, add 1 tbsp of the oil and fry half the mince until lightly browned. Remove the meat with a slotted spoon, letting the fat run back into the pan, then discard the fat. Add the remaining mince to the pan, brown it and drain off the fat in a similar way. Add the remaining oil and fry the chopped onion and carrot over a low heat for about 5 minutes until soft.

Stir in the dried thyme and flour, and cook for a few seconds, then add the beef stock and porter or stout. Bring to the boil and simmer until the gravy thickens. Tip the mince back in the pan, bring back to simmering point, then add the Worcestershire sauce and a little tomato ketchup for sweetness, if needed. Turn the heat right down and leave on a low heat for about half an hour. Check seasoning, adding salt and pepper to taste.

Meanwhile, put the potatoes in a saucepan, cover with cold water and bring to the boil. Cook for about 20 minutes until you can stick the point of a knife in them easily. Drain the potatoes, return them to the pan and cut them up roughly with a knife. Mash them thoroughly with a potato masher or fork. Beat in the butter and warm milk. Season with salt and pepper.

Preheat the grill. Tip the mince into a pie dish and spread the potato evenly over the top, roughing up the surface with a fork. Place the pie on a baking tray and grill for 5–10 minutes until the potato is nicely browned.

* You can assemble the pie in advance, refrigerate it, then bake it in a hot oven (200°C/400°F/Gas 6) for about 35–40 minutes.

Best beer match Good with the same beer you use in the recipe.

" At The Marquess, we stock Meantime's big chocolatey London Porter, which is based on a recipe from 1750 and includes seven different malts. We're big Meantime fans. The brewery was set up in 2000 in Greenwich by Alistair Hook, who admits that he scrounged money from friends, family and 'his parents' dog' to get it off the ground but it's played a significant part in reviving interest in beer. "

Great gravy

Gravy. If ever there were a more evocative food word, we've yet to come across it. And do you know what? Beer-based gravies are best of all. I've made gravies out of blonde ales (see page 69) and dark ales, out of classic British ales and big Belgian Trappist beers, out of household names like Newcastle Brown and Guinness, and obscure French artisanal beers. Without exception, they're all great, and hardly anyone spots that they've got beer in them either.

Gravy tips

* You need to start with some fat – about 2 tbsp to make enough gravy for 4. If you have a sticky, gooey, roasting pan, all the better, otherwise use a mixture of butter and a neutral cooking oil (not olive oil).

* You could add one or two sliced or chopped onions at this point. If you do, cook for about 10–15 minutes until soft and beginning to brown. Add a pinch of sugar towards the end to help the process.

* Stir in a tablespoon of plain flour and cook for a minute.

* Add 225ml (a mugful) of stock. Beef or Bovril stock (made with 1 tsp of Bovril) if you want a dark, meaty gravy; chicken stock if you want a lighter gravy for chicken or pork. A cube is fine (use half).

* Now add 150ml beer (do it this way round because you don't want it to bubble up fiercely or reduce too quickly, which will make the gravy bitter). You need a strong British ale or Belgian beer for a meaty gravy; a lighter blonde beer, Viennese lager or amber ale for pork or chicken (see page 69). Bring up to boiling point and simmer for about 5 minutes until the gravy becomes thick.

* Checking the seasoning is very important. If it's too sweet, add a few drops of cider or malt vinegar. If it's too bitter, add a little sugar, malt extract or tomato ketchup (a good old chef's trick). Too bland? A dash of brown sauce, Worcestershire sauce or madeira may help. Too strong? Add a little more beer, stock or water. Simply adjust it to your own personal taste.

Ham with Coke & stout

Having extolled the virtues of gravy, this recipe is actually nicer without it but it does make a truly fabulous stock that you can subsequently use to create a really dark sticky gravy for sausages (or, possibly even better, a black bean soup).

serves 4

1.2kg smoked gammon or bacon joint
660ml Guinness or Mackeson
660ml Coca-Cola
1 small onion, peeled and halved
3 tbsp dark molasses sugar
1½ tsp English mustard powder
¼ tsp sea salt
2–3 tsp malt vinegar

Soak the gammon in cold water for several hours or overnight. Put the joint in a deep saucepan that fits it snugly and pour in the Guinness and Coke, which should just about cover the ham. Add the onion and bring the liquid gradually to the boil. Turn the heat down to a bare simmer and cook for 1½ hours, turning the joint once during the cooking period and topping up with boiling water if necessary.

Remove the joint from the pan and reserve the stock. When the joint is cool enough to handle, cut away any rind. If you haven't already got the oven on for roast or baked potatoes, preheat it to 220°C/425°F/Gas 7.

Mix the molasses sugar, mustard powder and salt, and add enough malt vinegar to make a thick glaze. Put the gammon joint in a small roasting tin and brush with the glaze. Put a couple of spoonfuls of the cooking liquid in the tin to stop the glaze burning. Roast the joint for 10 minutes, basting with the glaze after 5 minutes, then turn the joint over, brush over the glaze and cook for another 5–10 minutes, basting again halfway through.

This is good served hot with roast or baked sweet potatoes or chips, or cold with potato salad.

Best beer match You can drink a stout or porter with this, although the sweet glaze may make it taste slightly bitter. We prefer a Trappist ale such as Westmalle Dubbel, Chimay Rouge or Orval, or a golden lager like Harviestoun Schiehallion.

Sausages

If ever there were a candidate for Ultimate Beer Food, it would have to be sausages. Sausage and mash, toad in the hole, sausages with lentils or beans like the Fabada overleaf, choucroute, hot dogs – they all go brilliantly with beer. Why? Well, it doesn't sound very appetizing but they're fatty and salty, two tastes that beer loves. And sometimes smoky, too. Bingo!

Some people like to bake or grill their sausages, but I don't think anything beats frying them slowly in a pan. And I mean slowly – about 15–20 minutes over a moderate heat. Pat them dry with kitchen towel so they brown properly, and don't prick them first or all the juices will run out.

Sausages & stoemp

This is a Belgian spin on sausages and mash. You can make stoemp with any kind of root vegetable or mix different kinds of greens in with it (spinach is popular), but I particularly like it with leeks. If you want to serve a gravy with this recipe, I suggest using a dark Trappist beer, such as Orval, as a base (see Gravy tips on page 98).

serves 3–4

12 plump traditional British sausages, slow-fried,
  as described above

for the stoemp:

650g boiling potatoes, peeled and quartered

250g turnips, peeled and cubed

1 tbsp sunflower or light olive oil

15g butter

1 large or 2 medium leeks, cleaned and sliced

1 tbsp crème fraîche or double cream (optional)

sea salt and freshly ground black pepper, to taste

Put the potatoes in a saucepan with the turnips, cover with cold water, bring to the boil and cook until tender (about 15–20 minutes). The turnips may take a little longer than the potatoes so cut them slightly smaller.

Drain thoroughly, return to the pan and mash with a potato masher and/or a fork until smooth.

Heat the oil in a frying pan, add the butter, then, once it has melted, add the leeks and stir-fry over a moderate heat until beginning to brown (about 4–5 minutes). Tip the leeks and butter into the mash along with the crème fraîche, if using, mix in well and season to taste with salt and freshly ground black pepper.

Serve with the slow-fried sausages.

Best beer match A dark Belgian Trappist ale like Orval or Chimay Rouge, or a Belgian brown ale.

" Bruin, brune or brown? Three different words for what can be three totally different ales. Bruin and brune are the Flemish and French words respectively for a strong, dark, dry slightly vinous ale, A British brown ale, on the other hand, is the bottled version of a dark mild, usually light in alcohol (3–3.5% ABV), mostly sweetish, like Manns Brown, and occasionally rich, malty and nutty, like Samuel Smith's Nut Brown Ale (5% ABV), a style that has been adopted by many brewers in the USA. "

Choucroute

This recipe came from a brilliantly quirky Alsace-themed restaurant called Schnecke in London's Soho, which, sadly, no longer exists. It makes a brilliant cheap, filling Sunday lunch with minimal effort on your part. What preparation there is can be done the day before.

serves 4–6

800g jar of sauerkraut

25g butter

75g pancetta cubes or chopped, smoked dry
  cured bacon

1 medium onion, roughly chopped

1 clove of garlic, crushed

1 large flavoursome eating apple, such as Cox or
  Blenheim, roughly chopped

5 juniper berries

¼ tsp caraway seeds/coriander seeds (optional)

3 cloves

a bouquet garni

freshly ground black pepper and a little nutmeg, to taste

150ml water

300ml dry riesling or a Czech lager like Budweiser Budvar

about 750g assorted smoked ham and sausages;
  if possible, include a couple of kabanos, some
  frankfurters and some kassler

Drain the sauerkraut and rinse in a large bowl of cold water. Repeat and drain again. Heat the butter in a casserole or large saucepan, add the pancetta or bacon, then, when the fat starts to run, add the chopped onion and garlic, and cook for about 5 minutes or until beginning to soften.

Add the apple, drained sauerkraut, spices and seasonings, water and wine or beer, bring to the boil, then cover and simmer slowly for an hour. Turn the heat off and leave for at least 4 hours or overnight.

Cut up the sausages and ham into large chunks and tuck in among the sauerkraut, then heat through slowly for another 45 minutes or until piping hot, turning the ingredients over a couple of times. Serve with Dijon mustard and plain boiled potatoes, sprinkled with parsley. Make sure that each person has a selection of the meats.

Best beer match Traditionally, this would be consumed with a light Alsace or German lager, but we favour a fuller Czech lager like Gambrinus or Budweiser Budvar.

Fabada

Beans and beer are a classic combination, and my version of this classic, Spanish-inspired stew makes a great dish for entertaining. Remember that you need to soak the beans beforehand.

serves 8

600g judion beans or butter beans

350g piece of smoked pancetta or a bacon hock

2 medium onions

1 stick of celery, trimmed and halved

1 carrot, peeled or scrubbed and halved

1 bay leaf

2–3 tbsp olive oil

350g cooking chorizo

350g morcilla (Spanish blood sausage) or black pudding

3 large cloves of garlic, peeled and crushed

2 tsp sweet smoked pimentón (mild Spanish paprika)

200g skinned, chopped fresh or tinned tomatoes

a pinch of saffron

sea salt and freshly ground black pepper, to taste

Soak the beans for at least 12 hours or overnight in cold water. Drain and put in a pan with the pancetta or bacon, one of the onions, peeled and halved, the celery, carrot and bay leaf. Cover with water and bring to the boil. Skim off any scum, turn the heat down, partly cover the pan and simmer for 1–2 hours until the beans are just cooked but not falling apart (beans vary considerably so keep an eye on them).

Meanwhile, heat a frying pan, add 2 tbsp of oil, brown the chorizo and morcilla lightly and set aside. Peel and roughly chop the remaining onion and fry in the oil until soft. Stir in the garlic and pimentón, and cook for a minute, then add the chopped tomatoes and 150ml of the bean cooking liquid (top the bean pan up with some more boiling water). Simmer for 15 minutes until the onions are tender.

Soak the saffron in 2 tbsp of the bean cooking liquid, then add to the tomatoes and onions. When the beans are cooked, remove the flavouring vegetables and the bacon.

Remove any skin or bone from the bacon and cut into chunks and return to the pan. Add the browned chorizo and morcilla sausages cut into three, and the tomato and onion mixture, and mix in with the beans.

Return to a very low heat to avoid the sausages breaking up and leave for another 30–45 minutes until the sausages are cooked and the beans well flavoured.

Season to taste with freshly ground black pepper and a little salt if necessary (it may be salty enough). Serve with a sharply dressed green salad.

Best beer match There's a great Spanish beer called Alhambra Reserva 1925 that would go perfectly with this, or try one of the artisanal beers from the Basque region of France like L'Amalthée.

spicy food

When we say spice we tend to think of food from the Indian sub-continent. Curry, in other words. But there are many other countries and regions that regularly incorporate spices in their cuisines: Mexico and the southern states of the US, Morocco, Thailand, China and the Caribbean all use spices in a slightly different way.

The common element in these cuisines is that dishes tend to be served at the same time, which makes pinpoint matching nigh on impossible. Not that it matters hugely. What we're looking for is a drink that can take on a range of different flavours, textures and temperatures.

Beer is ideal with spicy food for many reasons: its carbonation, which refreshes the palate; the moderate levels of alcohol; the absence of tannins and the presence of hops, which latch onto spices. The touch of sweetness in many beers helps, too.

The easiest way to decide which beer to drink is to think about the overall level of heat in the meal, although you can, of course, adjust the overall heat of a meal by bringing in milder dishes like dal or serving a cooling raita, chutney or salsa.

* Mild curries, such as kormas, or dry spiced dishes, such as tandoori chicken, pair well with wheat beers, golden ales and lagers, and pale ales.

* Medium-hot curries work particularly well with IPAs.

* Very hot curries slaughter practically everything. A light lager or a Kölsch is the best option.

* Chilli-hot dishes such as Singapore noodles or Szechuan beef can do with a touch more sweetness: try an American IPA or a blonde ale.

* Thai curries, which have an element of sourness, pair well with witbiers, bières blanches and similar aromatic wheat beers.

* Dishes with smoked chilli flavours, such as chilli con carne, work well with dark beers like brown ales and porters.

Beer & spicy snacks

Feel like a quiet night in with a good film? What could be better than a bottle or two of Pilsener, a good lager or IPA and some spicy Indian snacks?

This will give you all the components for a really satisfying TV dinner: hops, spice, crispy batter, the refreshing coolness and sourness of a raita or fresh coriander chutney. Perfect.

You can, of course, buy your snacks in – there are some great ones available at supermarkets or from takeaways, and I certainly wouldn't urge you to spend half a day making your own. But, if you've never made onion bhajias, for example, which are a world away from those solid footballs of dough you find in some Indian restaurants, do give them a try.

Crispy onion bhajias

These are much lighter than shop-bought onion bhajias and much more delicious, particularly if you heighten the onion flavour with crispy fried onions.

serves 4–6

2 medium onions, preferably organic, peeled and
  thinly sliced

1–2 green chillies, de-seeded and chopped

1 tsp cumin seeds

1 tsp all-purpose spice mix ✳

¾ tsp fine sea salt

25g dried crisp fried onions (you can buy these from
  Asian shops or in little tubs from supermarkets)

50g gram flour

50g plain flour

½ tsp baking powder

5–6 tbsp lager

1 tsp finely grated fresh ginger or ginger paste

vegetable or rapeseed oil for frying

Put the onions in a bowl with the chillies, cumin seeds, spice mix, salt and dried fried onions, and mix well. Sift the two flours together, then mix in the baking powder. Mix the flour into the onions, adding just enough lager to make a thick coating batter. Mix in the ginger.

Heat a wok, add the oil about ⅓ of the way up the pan and heat for about 2½–3 minutes until it will fry a cube of bread in a few seconds. Take dessertspoons of the mix and carefully drop them in the hot oil (you should be able to get five or six in the pan at one time). Flip them over once the underside is brown. Remove with a slotted spoon and drain briefly on kitchen towel.

Transfer to a warm plate and repeat with the rest of the mixture. Scatter over a little fresh coriander. Serve with fresh mint and coriander chutney (see right) or raita.

✳ This all-purpose spice mix can be used in any dish where you want a subtly spicy flavour. Mix 2 tsp each of ground coriander and cumin, ½ tsp turmeric and ¼ tsp chilli powder. It makes about 2 tbsp of seasoning.

Best beer match A witbier, bière blanche, Pilsener, golden lager or Cooper's Sparkling Ale.

Fresh mint & coriander chutney

The best-ever chutney to serve with spicy Indian snacks. Do buy your coriander and mint fresh from an Asian shop rather than in a supermarket pack. They're much better value and also have more flavour.

serves 4

½ a large bunch of fresh coriander

3–4 sprigs of fresh mint

2 slices of onion, roughly chopped

1 small clove of garlic, peeled and crushed (optional)

100ml natural yoghurt

1 tbsp freshly squeezed lemon juice

sea salt and cayenne pepper or chilli powder, to taste

Wash the coriander and cut away the stems (this should leave you with about 50g of leaves). Strip the leaves from the mint. Chop the leaves roughly, put in a blender or food processor with the onion, and whizz briefly until finely chopped. Add the garlic, if using, and yoghurt, and whizz till smooth. Season with the lemon, and salt and cayenne or chilli powder to taste.

Turn into a bowl, cover and refrigerate for half an hour to allow the flavours to amalgamate.

Cheat's chicken korma

There are so many really excellent Indian ready meals around that it doesn't seem worth making a curry from scratch, especially as authentic recipes often have a list of ingredients as long as your arm. I have a compromise, which is to base my recipes on one of the excellent curry pastes or sauces around now but add some extra ingredients that make the dish taste fresh and vibrant. In other words, I cheat. This is a punchier korma than you're probably used to but it is still quite mild and makes a simple mid-week supper.

serves 2

2–3 tbsp sunflower or other light cooking oil

½ a bunch of spring onions, trimmed and sliced
  into roughly 2cm lengths

2 skinless, boneless chicken breasts, about
  125–150g each

1 small onion, peeled and finely chopped

½ tsp coarse sea salt and 1 large clove of garlic,
  peeled and chopped, or 1 tsp garlic paste

1 tsp freshly grated ginger or ginger paste

2 tbsp korma paste or other mild curry paste

½ tsp ground turmeric (optional but good)

3 tbsp coconut cream or double cream

3 tbsp plain, stirred yoghurt or soy yoghurt

2 tbsp roughly chopped coriander

extra sea salt and lemon juice to taste, if needed

Heat 2 tbsp of the oil in a small frying pan and stir-fry the spring onions for a minute. Remove with a slotted spoon and set aside. Lightly brown the chicken breasts on each side and set them aside, too. Pour a little more oil into the pan and fry the chopped onion gently until soft.

Pound the garlic with the salt with a mortar and pestle until smooth and add the paste and the ginger to the onions, along with the korma paste and turmeric. Stir well, add 125ml of water, stir again, then return the chicken breasts to the pan. Spoon over the sauce, turn the heat down, cover the pan and simmer gently for about 25 minutes, until the chicken is cooked.

Remove the chicken from the pan and set aside. Add the coconut cream or double cream and yoghurt and stir well. Return the chicken pieces to the pan, along with the spring onions and roughly chopped coriander and heat through for a couple of minutes. Season with salt and lemon juice, if needed. Serve with boiled rice and peas and some naan bread.

**Best beer match A golden lager or a hoppy
pale ale, such as Marston's Pedigree.**

" Pale ale is a bottled version of bitter, which isn't pale as the name suggests but rich bronze or amber in colour. It tends to be slightly stronger than a draught bitter but not as strong and hoppy as an IPA. A typical British example is Marston's Pedigree, while the best-known American pale ale is Sierra Nevada. "

Rogan josh

Another short-cut but no one will know because this lamb curry tastes so authentic. If you can, make it the day before you want to eat it to give the flavours more time to develop.

serves 4–6, depending on how many other dishes you serve with it

750g shoulder of lamb, on or off the bone, cut into large pieces

2 tbsp sunflower or other light cooking oil

450g onions, peeled and sliced

2 cloves of garlic, peeled and finely chopped

1 tsp ground allspice

1/2 tsp ground cardamom (available from Asian grocers)

2 tsp sun-dried tomato paste

1 x 425g jar good-quality rogan josh sauce (I use Loyd Grossman's)

a few coriander stalks

sea salt, to taste

4 heaped tbsp natural yoghurt

2 heaped tbsp finely chopped coriander leaves

Remove any excess fat from the lamb (but not all of it – leave some for flavour). Heat a large frying pan, add the oil, heat for a couple of minutes, then fry the lamb pieces on all sides until lightly browned. Transfer to a casserole with a slotted spoon.

Fry the onions in the remaining oil until starting to soften, then add the garlic, turn the heat down, cover the pan and continue to cook until the onions are soft and caramelized (about 20 minutes). Add the allspice, cardamon and sun-dried tomato paste, then tip in the rogan josh sauce. Rinse the jar with a little hot water and add the contents to the pan as well, together with a few coriander stalks. Pour the sauce over the lamb, bring to the boil, stir, then turn the heat right down and leave to simmer for about 1 1/2 hours or until the lamb is tender. (You can make the Rogan josh ahead of time up to this point, leaving it to cool and reheating the next day.)

Before serving, check the seasoning, adding salt to taste if you feel it needs it. Spoon in the yoghurt and partially stir it into the curry. Scatter over a few chopped coriander leaves and serve with pilau rice, sag aloo (potato and spinach curry) and some onion or cucumber raita.

Best beer match This is perfect with an IPA (I paired it with one from the Meantime Brewery in Greenwich, which was great).

" It's no coincidence that IPAs go so well with curries. The beers got their name from the pale ales that were exported to India during the 19th century, which were made stronger and very highly hopped so that they would survive the long voyage. Today's IPAs don't have anything like the amount of hops that the Victorian ones would have done, but they are still significantly hoppier than a pale ale. "

Spicy duck noodles

This takes the ingredients of Chinese crispy duck, one of my favourite dishes, and turns them into a noodle dish.

serves 2

1 heaped tbsp hoisin sauce

2 cloves of garlic

1 tsp freshly grated ginger or ginger
  paste

225g duck breast fillets

20g dried shitake mushrooms

110g soba (buckwheat) noodles or wholewheat
  spaghetti broken in half to create short noodles

3–4 tbsp vegetable oil

a handful of shredded greens (spring greens or
  Brussels sprout tops)

½ a bunch of spring onions, trimmed and finely
  sliced

1 tbsp Japanese soy sauce (e.g. Kikkoman)
  + extra for serving

Mix the hoisin sauce with 2 tbsp of water, a crushed clove of garlic and grated ginger or ginger paste.

Cut the duck fillets into small strips and marinate in the sauce. Soak the mushrooms for 20 minutes in enough warm water to cover.

Bring a large pan of water to the boil and cook the noodles or spaghetti for a minute or so less than the time recommended on the pack, so they still have a little bite to them. Rinse with cold water and set aside.

Drain the mushrooms, strain the soaking water and set that aside, too. Finely slice the mushrooms.

Remove the duck from the marinade, shaking off any excess sauce. Heat a wok for a minute, add 2 tbsp of oil, then fry the finely sliced spring onions and greens for a minute or so until beginning to wilt. Remove from the pan.

Add a little more oil, then fry the duck and the mushrooms until the duck is lightly browned (about 2 minutes). Add the other clove of garlic, stir and return the greens and onions to the pan with the duck. Add the noodles, 1 tbsp of soy sauce, the remaining marinade and 2–3 tbsp of the mushroom soaking water and toss together lightly. Heat through for a couple of minutes, stirring occasionally, adding a little more of the mushroom water if the noodles start to catch.

Check the seasoning, adding extra soy sauce, if needed. Serve in deep bowls.

Best beer match **This would go really well with a dark Belgian abbey beer or an American brown ale.**

Thai green vegetable curry

Like the Cheat's chicken korma on page 108, this is an easy mid-week curry made with a paste, rather than from scratch. If you want to make more of an occasion out of the meal, start with the Spicy crab crostini on page 54.

serves 4

1 medium-sized aubergine
100g fine green beans
4 tbsp vegetable oil
1 medium onion, peeled and roughly
  chopped
2 cloves of garlic, peeled and crushed
1/2 a bunch of spring onions, trimmed and
  finely sliced *
2–3 tbsp home-made or shop-bought Thai
  green curry paste
1 x 400g tin of coconut milk
150g baby sweetcorn
100g sugar snap peas or frozen peas
2–3 tbsp natural yoghurt (optional)
4 heaped tbsp finely chopped fresh coriander
  leaves + a few extra leaves for decoration
4–5 lime leaves, finely shredded (optional)
juice of 1–2 limes (2–3 tbsp)
1–2 tsp light soy sauce, to taste
sea salt, for sprinkling and to taste

Trim the stalk off the aubergine and cut into cubes. Sprinkle with salt and leave for 30 minutes, then rinse well. Top and tail the beans and cut in half.

Blanch in boiling water for a minute, refresh with cold water and set aside.

Heat 3 tbsp of oil in a wok, add the cubed aubergine and stir-fry until lightly browned. Remove with a slotted spoon and set aside. Add a little extra oil to the pan and fry the onion until it begins to soften (about 4–5 minutes).

Add the crushed garlic and half the spring onions, stir in 2–3 tbsp Thai green curry paste (depending how hot you like your curry,) then pour in the coconut milk and stir again. Bring up to simmering point, add the blanched beans, sweetcorn and sugar snap peas and cook until tender (about 3–4 minutes).

Return the aubergine to the wok, along with the remaining spring onions, and heat through. Stir in the yoghurt, if using, fresh coriander and lime leaves, and season to taste with lime juice, soy sauce and a little salt, if you feel it needs it. Turn off the heat and leave for 5 minutes before serving with rice.

* For fine strips, trim the spring onions, cut them lengthways into halves or quarters, then cut three or four times across.

Best beer match **Belgian-style witbiers are sensational with Thai food.**

Lamb birria

An easy version of the birria served at Will's Mexican restaurant Green & Red – less authentic but still good! It's made with either chipotle en adobo, a kind of thick chilli compote, or chipotle ketchup, which is a smoother anglicized version. They're both available from Sainsbury's Special Selection range or from the Cool Chile Company in Borough Market, London, or online at www.coolchile.co.uk.

serves 4

4 lamb shanks

1 x 400g tin of whole tomatoes

1 large clove of garlic, peeled and crushed

1 tsp finely grated fresh ginger

1–2 tbsp chipotle ketchup or chipotle en adobo

150ml lager

a stick of cinnamon

1 bay leaf

2 tbsp dark muscovado sugar

sea salt, to taste

1/2 a small red onion, peeled and finely chopped

2 heaped tbsp chopped fresh coriander

for the marinade:

1 medium onion, peeled and roughly chopped

2 cloves of garlic, peeled and chopped

2 tbsp chipotle ketchup or chipotle en adobo

1–2 tbsp lager, if required

1 tsp ground cumin

1 tsp ground allspice

First, make the marinade. Put the onion and garlic in a blender with the chipotle ketchup or chipotle en adobo and whizz until smooth, adding a little lager if the mixture is too stiff to blend. Add the cumin and allspice and whizz again.

Pat the lamb shanks dry, put them in a large, lidded casserole and pour over the marinade and rub it in well.

Cover the lamb shanks and leave for at least an hour, preferably two. Preheat the oven to 190°C/375°F/Gas 5.

Tip the tomatoes, garlic and ginger for the sauce into the blender. Add 1–2 tbsp of chipotle ketchup or chipotle en adobo, depending on how hot you want the dish to be, then add the lager and whizz briefly again. Tip the sauce over the lamb shanks, add the cinnamon stick, bay leaf and sugar, stir, cover the pan and bake in the oven for 20 minutes. Turn the heat down to 150°C/300°F/Gas 2 and cook for another 2–2 1/2 hours, occasionally turning the lamb shanks and spooning over the sauce.

Remove the pan from the heat, remove the lamb shanks, let the sauce cool for 10 minutes or so, then skim off the fat. (Alternatively, leave the lamb shanks in the pan, cool the dish completely, leave overnight and remove the fat the following day.)

Return the lambshanks to the pan, spoon over the sauce, reheat gently and cook for another 45 minutes to an hour until the meat begins to fall off the bone. Season to taste with salt, and scatter over the finely chopped red onion and fresh coriander.

Serve with corn tortillas, refried beans and a shredded cabbage salad.

Best beer match A Negra Modelo or other Viennese-style lager.

" A Mexican restaurant needs two things: tequila and Mexican beer. At Green & Red, we have 190 of the former but had to settle for slightly fewer of the latter! We didn't want to go overboard on Pilseners, although Mexico has many of them, so we limited them to Sol and Bohemia, then set about trying to convert people to more flavoursome beers like Dos XX and Negra Modelo (a Viennese-style lager). We did find a cool little microbrewery called Casta, which made fantastic ales. Unfortunately, they are no longer available in this country, which goes to show you can sometimes get thwarted when you try to serve good beer. "

Real chile

I've had a bit of a fixation with chile (the Spanish and American way of spelling chilli) since going to Santa Fe a few years ago. There they have a special type of chile called New Mexico Red, or chile Colorado. It has a distinctively smoky, earthy flavour, which makes it go really well with dark beers. The nearest equivalent is not the mild chilli powder we find here but Spanish pimentón, which is similarly roasted and ground. If you want to make a really good chile con carne (a Tex Mex version), do try to get hold of some.

Chile Colorado   I wouldn't claim this as an authentic American Southwest chile but if you've only ever made a basic chile con carne, you'll be amazed at the taste. The two big differences are that the meat is chopped rather than minced, and the amount of chile used gives the sauce an incredible richness and depth that cries out for a good beer.

serves 6

for the beans:

250g dried red kidney beans

1 bay leaf

a few black peppercorns

1 tsp epazote (Mexican herb)
 – optional

for the chile:

1kg braising steak

5–6 tbsp sunflower or other light cooking oil

2 onions (about 250g in total), peeled and
 roughly chopped

3 cloves of garlic, peeled and crushed

1 heaped tbsp tomato paste

1 level tbsp plain flour
5–6 tbsp chile molido (mild New Mexican ground chile ✱)
1½ tsp ground cumin
300ml beef stock
175ml lager
1 tbsp cider vinegar
sea salt and freshly ground black pepper, to taste

Soak the beans overnight in cold water. Drain them, cover with fresh cold water and bring to the boil. Skim off any scum and boil hard for 10 minutes, then turn the heat down and add the bay leaf, peppercorns, epazote, if using (it flavours the beans and causes less flatulence!).

Cook for about 1–1¼ hours until the beans are tender, topping up with boiling water as necessary. Set aside until the chile is cooked.

Meanwhile, pat the meat dry, remove any fat or gristle and cut into very small cubes. Pour a little of the oil into a frying pan and brown the meat in batches, transferring it to a casserole as you complete each batch. Add the remaining oil (you'll need about 3 tbsp) and fry the onions until soft but not coloured. Add the crushed garlic, cook for a minute, then stir in the tomato paste, flour, 5 tbsp of the chile powder and the cumin.

Cook for a few seconds, then add the stock and lager and bring to the boil. Pour the sauce over the meat, stir well, bring back to the boil, then turn the heat right down and simmer for 2–3 hours until the meat is tender, adding a little water if the sauce gets too thick.

Drain the beans and add to the meat and cook for another half hour. Taste the sauce and add 1 tbsp of cider vinegar and a little more chile powder just to lift the flavour. Season with salt and black pepper to taste.

Serve with warm corn or wheat tortillas and a salsa like the avocado salsa (see right).

✱ Try www.coolchile.co.uk or www.thespiceshop.co.uk for chile molido. Alternatively, use a combination of mild chilli powder and hot and sweet Spanish pimentón.

Best beer match We like this with a smoked ale or a porter but it would also be good with an American IPA or American brown ale.

Avocado salsa   This is probably the salsa I make the most often. It's also great with seared tuna.

500g tomatoes
½ a bunch of spring onions
2 ripe avocados
juice of 1–2 limes
3 tbsp roughly chopped fresh coriander
sea salt and freshly ground black pepper, to taste

Skin and roughly chop the tomatoes.✱ Trim the spring onions, cut lengthways, then slice finely. Peel and cube the avocados. Mix together and pour over the lime juice. Season with salt and pepper. Mix in the fresh coriander just before serving.

✱ To skin tomatoes, make a small nick in the skin by the stem. Put the tomatoes in a bowl and pour over boiling water. Leave for a minute, then drain and pour over cold water. The skins should slip off easily.

Joloffe rice

This is my spin on a popular West African rice dish that isn't a million miles from paella. Some versions include dried shrimps but, as these are both difficult to get hold of and quite salty, I suggest using crayfish tails or ordinary prawns and a dash of Thai fish sauce (nam pla) instead.

serves 6

1 tbsp sunflower or other light cooking oil

100g chunk of chorizo, skinned and cut into small dice

3–4 boned, skinless chicken thighs, cut into chunks (about 350g in total)

1 medium onion, peeled and roughly chopped

1 medium red pepper, de-seeded and chopped

1 medium green pepper, de-seeded and chopped

2 cloves of garlic, peeled and very finely chopped

2 tsp jerk seasoning

1 tsp turmeric

½ tsp sweet smoked pimentón (mild Spanish paprika)

½ x 400g tin of chopped tomatoes

600ml hot stock made with 2 tsp vegetable bouillon or a chicken or vegetable stock cube

250g Spanish bomba or Calasparra rice

175g crayfish tails or prawns, drained, halved and macerated with 1 tsp Thai fish sauce (nam pla)

3 heaped tbsp chopped parsley

freshly ground black pepper, to taste

Heat a wok and add 1 tbsp of oil. Tip in the chorizo and stir for a minute, then add the chicken and stir-fry for a few minutes until the chicken is lightly coloured.

Remove the chorizo and chicken from the pan with a slotted spoon and set aside. Add an extra spoonful of oil to the pan and add the onion and chopped peppers. Stir-fry for about 4 or 5 minutes until they start to soften and brown. Stir in the garlic and spices, cook for a minute, then return the chicken and chorizo to the pan. Add the rice, stir, then add the tomatoes, breaking them down well with a wooden spoon. Pour in the stock. Turn the heat down and cook the rice gently for about 15–20 minutes, giving an occasional stir to stop the rice sticking to the base of the pan (but don't stir it like a risotto).

When the liquid is almost absorbed, add the prawns and cook for a further 4 or 5 minutes until there is no liquid left. Season with freshly ground black pepper (you shouldn't need salt), stir in the parsley, then cover the pan and leave for 5 minutes for the flavours to be absorbed and the rice to fluff up.

Best beer match A light hoppy British bitter (I drank Badger's Fursty Ferret with it, which was surprisingly good), an amber or ambrée ale, or a Viennese-style lager.

salads & veg

The time is thankfully long gone when salad meant a few limp lettuce leaves topped with a couple of slices of tomato and cucumber and some vinegary beetroot gradually turning the salad cream magenta-pink. Salads can consist of virtually anything these days, and many have ingredients that make them particularly beer-friendly: croutons, crisp-fried bacon, sautéed chicken livers, wafer-thin slices of Parmesan or other cheeses, cured meats like ham and salami, seafood and smoked fish, chargrilled vegetables, potatoes, nuts and pulses like lentils and beans... the list is endless.

Beer works well with raw vegetables because of its effervescence, providing a refreshing accompaniment that won't overwhelm delicate flavours. It's even better than wine with bitter or salty ingredients such as raw onion, anchovies or capers. If you're looking for a match with cold meats and coleslaw, go for a beer!

Just as with any other type of food, it helps when you're matching vegetable-based dishes to focus on the overall style of a dish and identify the dominant ingredients. However, in general:

* Spring vegetable-based dishes, such as risottos and pasta dishes with creamy sauces, pair well with witbiers and light Pilseners.

* Mediterranean vegetables, such as aubergines, courgettes and tomatoes, work well with amber ales and lagers.

* Roast root vegetables, like onions, carrots, parsnips and swede, are great with hearty British ales or strong Belgian beers.

* Mushrooms, particularly dishes with flavoursome portabello or field mushrooms, suit dark beers and lagers, which also work well with beetroot-based dishes.

* Sweet-tasting vegetables, such as red and yellow peppers, pumpkin or squash, are good matches with strong golden and blonde ales and American IPAs.

* Dark green vegetables, such as broccoli, spinach and cabbage, are usually combined with another ingredient, such as eggs, cheese or sausages. This will obviously influence the beer match, but golden ales or lagers are usually a pretty safe bet.

Beer & salad dressings

Just as your choice of beer with pasta or chicken is determined by the sauce you serve with it, the choice of beer with a salad depends on the dressing. Some, like the Soy & sesame dressing below, work well with beer; others, like the raspberry and honey dressing with the Smoked duck salad on page 78, can be based on beer (fruit beers and sharp-flavoured beers like gueuze are particularly well suited to this).

The key points to remember when making a dressing with beer are not to use too assertively flavoured an oil (grapeseed oil is perfect), to use rather more beer than you would normally vinegar (about 40–50% of the total mixture) and to sweeten the dressing slightly to counteract any hop bitterness (honey works especially well with fruit beers).

Piquant salad dressing
This makes a good dressing for a salad that's to be served with tuna or with cold jellied meats like brawn, fromage de tête and jambon persillé.

enough to dress a salad for 3–4

1/4 tsp English mustard powder or Dijon mustard

sea salt, freshly ground black pepper and a pinch
  of sugar

4 tbsp oude gueuze

4 tbsp light olive oil

1 tbsp very finely chopped red onion

1 tsp capers, rinsed and finely chopped

2 gherkins or cornichons, rinsed and finely chopped

1 tbsp finely chopped fresh parsley

sea salt and freshly ground black pepper, to taste

Put the seasonings in a bowl or screw-topped jar, add the gueuze and whisk or shake together. Whisk in the oil or add the oil and shake again. Add the chopped onion, capers, gherkins and parsley and whisk or shake once more. Check for seasoning.

Soy & sesame salad dressing
This oriental-inspired dressing goes particularly well with two contrasting styles of beer: IPAs and witbiers.

enough to dress a salad for 4

2 tbsp organic sunflower oil

2 tbsp seasoned rice vinegar

2 tsp light soy sauce

1–2 drops (no more!) sesame oil

Simply whisk the ingredients together or shake them together in a screw-topped jar.

" The dressings that go well with beer include mustardy vinaigrettes and creamy dressings, like those used on the Emmental salad (see page 124) and on the Chicken Caesar salad (see page 76). Blue cheese dressings actually go better with beer than with wine – a burger with salad and a blue cheese dressing is a fine match for a brown ale. Oriental-influenced dressings also work well, especially those with a nutty sesame note (see above). "

Emmental, fennel & apple salad with honey, mustard & yoghurt dressing

Emmental is a useful cheese in a salad because it doesn't break up. The addition of apple and fennel and a light yoghurt dressing makes a particularly fresh, summery combination.

serves 4 as a starter or 2 as a main course

2 Little Gem lettuce hearts

200g Emmental cheese

1 small to medium bulb of fennel (about 200g) with
   leaves (if there are no leaves, you'll need a couple of
   sprigs of fresh dill)

1 medium-sized Braeburn apple

for the dressing:

1 tsp Dijon mustard

1 tsp clear honey

1 tbsp cider vinegar

3 tbsp grapeseed oil or light olive oil

100ml low fat natural stirred yoghurt

fine sea salt and freshly ground black pepper,
   to taste

Trim the base off the lettuce hearts, break off the
leaves and put them in a large bowl of iced water to
crisp up.

Next, prepare the dressing. Measure the mustard,
honey and cider vinegar into a bowl and whisk
together with a fork or hand whisk. Gradually add the
oil, whisking as you go until you have a thick dressing.
Mix in the yoghurt and season to taste with salt and
freshly ground black pepper.

Remove any rind off the cheese and cut into bite-
sized pieces.

Trim the green stalks and any leaves off the fennel and
set aside. Cut the fennel in half and slice thinly. Drain
the lettuce leaves and pat them dry with a clean tea
towel or some kitchen towel.

Quarter and core the apple. Line a large bowl with
the lettuce leaves and then layer up the other
ingredients starting with the cheese, followed by the
fennel and then the apple, cut into slices directly onto
the salad (this prevents it discolouring). Give the
dressing a final whisk, pour over the salad and top
with the reserved finely chopped fennel leaves and
stalks. Toss at the table before serving.

∗ To make this recipe more substantial, you could
add about 150g thick-cut ham off the bone, diced
or in strips.

Best beer match This summery dish needs
a light summer ale, such as Badger's Golden
Champion, or a honey beer, like Young's
Waggle Dance.

" Honey beer contains a hell of a lot of honey – as much as 20% of the brew. And honey,
I am led to believe, is an aphrodisiac, which would suggest that if you're trying to seduce
someone, this may well be the beer to pour... "

sausages & potato salad

It's pretty hard to go anywhere in Bavaria, especially round Oktoberfest time, without encountering a sausage. Or a potato salad. Or, quite frequently, both.

There are a multitude of different types of sausages and other cold meats to be found in Germany, as you'll discover in any supermarket or deli. Those good for eating cold include bierwurst, which, oddly, doesn't include beer but is simply good with it, blutwurst (blood sausage) and schinkenwurst (ham sausage). Other popular products are Münchener leberkäse (a sort of meat loaf), haxensülze (a jellied brawn, flavoured with caraway), Schweinsbraten (roast pork) and, of course, the famous Schwarzwälder schinken (black forest ham). All are great with a helles beer – and a potato salad, of course.

Bavarian potato salad

During the Oktoberfest, I became quite obsessed with potato salads with their refreshing sweet–sour flavour and wonderfully gooey consistency. (I later discovered that this came from hot stock.) I had to try potato salads everywhere we went until I cracked the secret of how to make them, as revealed below.

serves 4–6

1kg of waxy new potatoes, peeled and cut into
  even-sized pieces

1 tsp vegetable bouillon powder

4 tbsp white malt vinegar

½ tsp sea salt

½ tsp caster sugar

¼ tsp white pepper

2 tbsp sunflower or grapeseed oil

1 medium-sized mild or sweet onion, peeled and
  finely chopped

40g butter

fresh chives or dill

Put the potatoes in a pan, cover with cold water and bring to the boil. Simmer until tender – about 12–15 minutes. Drain, reserving the cooking water.

Pour 150ml of the cooking water over the vegetable bouillon powder and stir. When the potatoes are cool enough to handle (about 5 minutes), slice them roughly into a bowl. Put the vinegar in a small saucepan. Add the salt, caster sugar and pepper, and stir to dissolve. Add the oil and the onion, bring to the boil, then pour the hot dressing and stock over the sliced potatoes, and stir.

Melt the butter, add to the salad and stir again. Add a little more of the potato cooking water, stirring vigorously, to give a slightly sloppy consistency. Leave to cool and stand for about 2 hours for the flavours to develop. Sprinkle with snipped chives or finely chopped dill and serve with cold sliced sausage and ham or with grilled bratwurst.

* Sometimes the locals add cucumber to their potato salad. Take half a cucumber, peel it, halve it and scoop out the seeds with the tip of a teaspoon. Cut into slices, put on a shallow plate, sprinkle with sea salt and put another weighted plate on top. Leave for about 20 minutes, then rinse the cucumber and pat dry. Dress with a little white vinegar, seasoned as above with sea salt, caster sugar, white pepper and a splash of sunflower oil.

Best beer match Given this is a Münchener salad, you should drink an authentic Münchener helles or weissbier with it – or, at a pinch, a Czech golden lager.

Japanese-style winter vegetable stew with miso

With its sweet/savoury flavour, miso is a product that goes really well with beer, and this hearty Japanese-style root vegetable stew is a great way to serve it. You can obviously vary the vegetables, depending on what's available, but keep it colourful. You'll need about 1.25kg of veg in total, preferably organic.

serves 4–6

3 tbsp sunflower oil or other light cooking oil

1 medium onion, peeled and roughly chopped

2 carrots, peeled and thickly sliced (about 250g)

1 parsnip, peeled and chopped into largeish cubes (about 200g)

½ a small swede or two turnips, peeled and cut into cubes (about 250g)

1 clove of garlic, peeled and finely chopped

750ml light vegetable stock made with 1 organic vegetable stock cube or 1 tbsp vegetable bouillon powder

3–4 Jerusalem artichokes (about 200g)

1 sweet potato, peeled and cut into largeish cubes

2 tsp brown miso paste

a dash of Japanese soy sauce (about 1 tsp)

freshly ground black pepper

a handful of chives

Heat the oil in a lidded casserole. Add the chopped onion, carrots, parsnip and swede, stir well, cover the pan and cook on a low heat for about 10–15 minutes until the vegetables start to soften. Add the chopped garlic, stir and cook for a couple more minutes, then pour in the stock. Bring to the boil and cook, uncovered, for another 5 minutes or so.

Peel the Jerusalem artichokes and slice them thickly into the pan, add the cubed sweet potato and carry on cooking until all the vegetables are tender (about another 15 minutes).

Take the pan off the heat. Spoon the miso into a cup, add about 4 tbsp of the hot stock from the vegetables and stir to dissolve the paste. Tip the liquid back into the stew and mix in thoroughly. Add a little soy sauce and some freshly ground black pepper. Serve in bowls, scattering over a few snipped chives.

Beer match A Belgian brune beer is a perfect accompaniment but a German dunkel or an amber ale would also go well.

" Dunkel is one of those vague beer words that doesn't give you much of a clue about the taste of the beer in the bottle because it simply means dark. But for the most part it is applied to lagers that are made from dark roasted malts. It is a style traditionally common in Bavaria and the Czech Republic, but more recently it has become popular in the United States. "

Welsh rabbit leeks

This is my adaptation of a great idea from cookery writer and top London chef Mark Hix – pouring a Welsh rarebit, or should I say rabbit, over cooked leeks.

serves 2–3

6 even-sized leeks (about 500g in total)

5 tbsp full-bodied English ale, such as Ridley's Old Bob

150g strong Cheddar cheese, grated

1 level tbsp plain flour sifted with ½ level tsp
English mustard powder

1 large egg yolk

1½ tbsp Worcestershire sauce

3 tbsp double cream

freshly ground black pepper

Trim the leeks, removing any damaged outer leaves. Cut vertically halfway down each leek, fan out the leaves and rinse under cold running water to remove any grit. Cut the leeks across in half and arrange in the basket of a steamer. Steam for about 4–5 minutes until just cooked.

Pour the ale into a saucepan, add the cheese, sprinkle over the sifted flour and mustard, and stir. Heat over a low heat until the cheese has melted and formed a smooth sauce.

Take off the heat and beat in the egg yolk, then add

the Worcestershire sauce and cream. Season with plenty of freshly ground black pepper (you shouldn't need salt).

Heat the grill. Arrange the leeks in a baking dish and pour over the rarebit. Place the dish under the grill for about 2–3 minutes until brown and bubbling.

Serve with crusty bread.

Best beer match **Drink the same beer that you use for the recipe.**

Rarebit or rabbit?   It's rabbit, according to Alan Davidson's *Oxford Companion to Food*, the faintly insulting idea being that cheese was all the protein the Welsh could afford. Rarebit became popular as a clearer indication of the nature of the dish, which is obviously not related to rabbit at all. Beer is a common but not invariable addition – some cooks use milk instead.

Aubergine parmigiana

This is one of those very simple recipes that depends on good ingredients, especially the cheese. Normally, I'd make it with ordinary mozzarella, but smoked mozzarella (mozzarella di bufala affumicate) gives it a smoky edge that's a better match for beer. It's good as a light lunch served with crusty bread and a green salad.

serves 2

1 large aubergine
2 tbsp olive oil
1 clove of garlic, peeled and crushed
200g best-quality Italian tinned tomatoes
a pinch of dried oregano (optional)
125g smoked or ordinary buffalo mozzarella
sea salt, sugar and freshly ground black
  pepper

Wipe the aubergine, cut off the stalk, then cut a slice off each of the long sides. Cut the remaining flesh vertically into four long even-sized slices. Lay them out on a work surface or chopping board, sprinkle them with salt and leave them for 20–30 minutes. Rinse the salt off and pat them dry.

Meanwhile, make the tomato sauce. Heat 1 tbsp of the olive oil in a frying pan over a medium heat, add the crushed garlic and stir for a couple of seconds. Tip in the tomatoes and break them down with a wooden spoon, spatula or fork. Add the dried oregano if using, stir and cook quite fast for 5 minutes until most of the liquid has disappeared. Season lightly with

salt, pepper and a little sugar and tip into a bowl. Rinse and dry the pan.

Slice the mozzarella into fine slices. Preheat the oven to 220°C/425°F/Gas 7.

Drizzle a little olive oil over both sides of each aubergine 'steak' and rub it in with your fingers. Heat the pan and, when it's almost smoking, put the aubergine slices in and sear them briefly on both sides. (You may have to do this in two batches.) Lay them on a baking sheet and spoon 1 tbsp of tomato sauce over each one, then top with mozzarella slices.

Trickle over a little extra olive oil and bake for about 7–8 minutes until the aubergines are heated through and the cheese has melted.

Best beer match **An amber ale or lager would be our top choice but an American- or Belgian-style brown ale would be pretty good, too.**

Mushroom moussaka

This is moussaka only in the very loosest sense – it doesn't contain lamb or aubergine but merely has a custardy, moussaka-like topping, and even that isn't made in the conventional way! But it's very tasty indeed and makes a good main course to serve to veggie and non-veggie friends alike.

serves 4–6

2 tbsp sunflower oil or other light cooking oil

1 large onion, peeled and finely chopped

2 cloves of garlic, peeled and crushed

500g chestnut mushrooms, wiped and quartered

200g chopped tinned tomatoes

2 tbsp sun-dried tomato paste or ordinary tomato paste

a pinch of cinnamon

½ tsp dried oregano

½ x 400g tin black-eye beans, drained and rinsed

sea salt and freshly ground black pepper, to taste

for the topping:

300ml crème fraîche

3 large eggs, lightly beaten

25g freshly grated Parmesan cheese

Heat the oil in a wok or large frying pan and fry the onion over a moderate heat until beginning to soften (about 3–4 minutes). Add the garlic, stir and cook for a minute, then add the mushrooms. Cook, stirring occasionally for about 5–6 minutes until just cooked and most of the liquid released by the mushrooms is absorbed.

Stir in the tomatoes and sun-dried or ordinary tomato paste, add the cinnamon and oregano, then add the black-eye beans. Season to taste with salt and freshly ground black pepper. Tip the mixture into a lightly oiled ovenproof dish and leave to cool for at least half an hour.

Heat the oven to 190°C/375°F/Gas 5. Measure out the crème fraîche into a large jug. Beat in the eggs about a third at a time, then add the Parmesan. Season with salt and pepper.

Pour the custard over the mushrooms and beans, and bake for about 40–45 minutes until the topping is lightly set, golden and puffy. Serve with a green salad.

Best beer match We'd go for a dunkel or dubbel beer with this recipe – always a good match for mushrooms.

bread & cheese

If you asked a teetotaller or someone who had never drunk beer what food they thought beer went best with, they would almost certainly say bread and cheese. Whether it's a ploughman's, a cheese and pickle sandwich or cheese on toast, they're all great matches for real ale.

Beer has, of course, been used in the bread-making process for centuries, particularly in England where bakers preferred to use barm (the froth of fermenting liquor) from beer to start their loaves, rather than a sourdough starter reliant on wild yeasts. As Dan Lepard explains in his fascinating book **The Handmade Loaf** (Mitchell Beazley, 2004), the mild antiseptic properties of hops stops the starter from souring. He suggests using a live bottled-conditioned ale to make a modern version of the barm, heating it to 70°C (160°F), then whisking in strong white flour, cooling it, then adding in your own leaven. My husband, who's a keen bread-maker, has recently been converted to the technique but you do need to have some kind of sourdough starter going.

Those of you who are more casual bread-makers, like me, may enjoy the easy sunflower seed bread recipe on page 136, which is an excellent partner for beer. I had previously made this recipe without beer but found that the stout not only boosted the very short rising period but gave the bread an extra richness and depth of flavour.

Beer and cheese, of course, is almost a book on its own and an endless source of pleasurable experimentation. Unlike fine wine, which frequently fights the world's most interesting artisanal cheeses, you can almost always find a beer that will match harmoniously – and at considerably less expense. Beer, bread and cheese is really one of life's most affordable luxuries.

Sunflower seed & stout bread

An adaptation of a fabulous mixed seed bread that I discovered in South Africa but made even better by the addition of beer. It also has the huge advantage that it doesn't require kneading – all you need do is simply mix the ingredients and wait for it to rise.

425g organic malthouse or granary flour

75g oatmeal bran

50g sunflower seeds + extra for topping

15g each poppy and sesame seeds + extra
   for topping

1½ tsp fine sea salt

1 tbsp barley malt extract (available from health
   food stores)

1 heaped tbsp liquid molasses, dark molasses sugar,
   treacle or honey

150ml sweet stout, such as Mackeson

1½ tsp easy blend yeast

1 tbsp organic sunflower oil + extra for
   greasing the tin

You will need a 900g bread tin, preferably non-stick

Tip the flour, bran, seeds and salt into a large bowl and mix together well. (If your flour is cold, warm it in the microwave for 30 seconds.) Measure 300ml of hand hot water into a jug and stir in the barley malt extract and molasses or treacle or honey. Add the stout.

Sprinkle the yeast over the flour mix and form a hollow. Pour in 2/3 of the beer liquid and the oil, and stir with a wooden spoon, gradually adding as much extra liquid as the flour will absorb. (The consistency should be wetter than a normal loaf – more like that of a fruitcake.) Keep stirring until the dough begins to come away from the sides of the bowl (about 2 minutes).

Tip the dough into a well-greased bread pan, pressing it down evenly. Cover with clingfilm or a damp cloth, and leave to rise for about 25–30 minutes until the surface of the loaf is about 2cm from the top of the tin.

Meanwhile, heat the oven to 200°C/400°F/Gas 6. Gently brush the top of the loaf with lightly salted water, then spoon or shake the seeds in 3 vertical lines down the length of the bread to give you a stripy topping. Bake in the oven for about 40 minutes.

Using a round-bladed knife, loosen the sides of the loaf away from the sides of the tin, then carefully ease it out and return the loaf to the oven for a final 5 minutes for the base to crisp up. Take the loaf from the oven and leave on a cooling rack until completely cold. Leave it for a couple more hours to firm up before slicing.

This bread is particularly good with a soft, fresh goats' cheese, a strong Cheddar or a creamy blue.

My perfect ploughman's

I always think we're kidding ourselves if we imagine a ruddy-cheeked ploughman, sitting under a tree on a balmy summer's day, tucking into a home-baked loaf and a chunk of Cheddar, washed down with a foaming flask of ale. As Laura Mason and Catherine Brown point out in their *Traditional Foods of Britain* (Prospect Books, 1999), 'there is no evidence that such a combination was commonly eaten by ploughmen in the past or that ploughmen ate lunch in the modern sense of the word'.

However, there's no doubt that a ploughman's has become a staple of the British pub lunch – or, regrettably, that you can put together a very much better one yourself than the average publican. Exactly what goes into a ploughman's is open to dispute (and you can see Will's views on what consitutes a perfect ploughman's on page 171). For me, it should include a freshly baked white cottage loaf with a really good

crisp crust and a good piece of mature artisanal farmhouse Cheddar or, at a pinch, Lancashire cheese (I don't like a selection of cheeses – that's a cheeseboard). Some ham is not unwelcome but it must be freshly and thickly cut off the bone, not from a pre-sliced pack.

Most controversially, I don't like pickled onions, which seem invariably too sharp and can have an unpredictable effect on the beer. The beer-glazed onions below are much sweeter, mellower and easier to make than a home-made chutney, though that is good as well. I certainly don't want an outsized spring onion (again too harsh and sour for many beers) but a few home-grown tomatoes go down rather well in season.

As far as the beer is concerned, it mustn't be anything but British. I'm particularly partial to a Timothy Taylor's Landlord or a Thornbridge Jaipur IPA.

Beer & balsamic-glazed onions to go with a ploughman's

This is a much milder, sweeter condiment than the traditional pickled onions, and it goes particularly well with classic British or British-style ales.

serves 6

2 tbsp sunflower, grapeseed or vegetable oil

500g medium-sized onions, peeled and cut into 8 wedges

2 tbsp demerara sugar

5 tbsp (75ml) brown ale, such as Manns

4 tbsp apple balsamic vinegar

a few black peppercorns (about 7–8)

1 bay leaf

Heat the oil in a heavy-bottomed saucepan, add the onions, stir well and turn the heat down low. Cover the pan and cook for about 15 minutes, stirring the onions occasionally until they start to soften.

Add the sugar, stir and cook for a couple of minutes, then pour in the brown ale and apple balsamic vinegar. Add the peppercorns and bay leaf, bring to the boil and simmer over a low heat for about 25 minutes until the onions are tender.

Turn the heat up and cook fast until all the liquid has evaporated. Cool and refrigerate. Bring to room temperature before using.

" Unlike Mum, I love pickles with ploughman's – pickled onions, piccalilli, pickled anything. The whole point for me is an assault of different flavours and pairings on the plate. So my perfect ploughman's would be a huge hunk of white bread, meat (plenty of it, especially ham off the bone), strong-flavoured English cheese, ripe tomatoes, pickles galore and something green and crunchy, like raw spring onions. To drink, I like a full-flavoured, hoppy beer, like Young's Champion, or a genuinely bitter ale, like Hop Back Summer Lightning. "

Which beer, which cheese?

A few years ago, I did a couple of major tastings with London's leading cheesemonger, Patricia Michelson of La Fromagerie, looking at how different cheeses paired with different drinks. I was really impressed by how much easier it was to match cheese with beer than with wine. It's not an opinion I've subsequently had cause to revise.

Sure, there are exceptions. It's easy enough to match a fresh, young goats' cheese with a sauvignon blanc, or a sweet wine like port with a Stilton, but mature artisanal cheeses, the kind that cheese lovers worship, are notoriously tricky with wine, and red wine in particular.

Which beers best match which cheeses depends on your own personal taste, the state of the cheese on the day or how many different cheeses you're calling on the beer to tackle. However, here are some guidelines that should prove useful.

* Mild cheeses, such as goats' cheese, and mild British territorial cheeses, such as Caerphilly and Wensleydale
A strong ale will easily overwhelm this style of cheese but a witbier, bière blanche or similar light cloudy wheat beer is perfect.

* Semi-soft white-rinded cheeses, such as Brie and Camembert
As with many cheeses, this depends on how runny you let them get but, generally, golden ales and lagers are a reliable bet, while berry-flavoured fruit beers, such as kriek and frambozen, are outstanding.

* Cheddar and other full-flavoured British hard cheeses
There's a division of opinion here. There are those who claim there's nothing better than an IPA, but I find some British IPAs can get overpowered by a strong Cheddar. An American IPA, maybe, but we prefer a good British ale, like Young's Special or Fuller's 1845, or the oak-aged Innis & Gunn. A lightly smoked ale, an American brown ale or a Belgian brune can also be good.

* Gouda-style cheeses
If mature (and it's not really worth eating these cheeses otherwise), try Belgian Trappist ale, like Orval or – the ultimate match, according to Garrett Oliver of the Brooklyn Brewery – a saison.

* Sheep's cheeses, such as Manchego, those from the Pyrenees and Berkswell
Good, as you'd expect, with artisanal French and Spanish beers from the Basque country, many of which tend to be amber in style. Viennese-style lagers and pumpkin ales (on a similar basis to the quince paste membrillo) will work, too, as will a dark mild.

* Washed-rind cheeses, such as Epoisses, Maroilles and Stinking Bishop
These cheeses have their rind brushed with brine, wine, beer or cider as they mature, creating a strong, pungent rind and an unctuously rich interior, which makes them notoriously difficult to match with wine. Strong Trappist ales, such as Chimay Bleu or a French bière de garde, are a much better pairing.

* Alpine cheeses, such as Gruyère, Comté, Beaufort
A good match with a powerfully flavoured beer. I had an artisanal French smoked beer called La Rouget de Lisle Vieux Tuyé with a Comté recently – a great pairing. Garrett Oliver (see above) swears by Gruyère with doppelbock. Other dark ales should work, too.

* Blue cheeses
Two possibilities: porter, which goes particularly well with Stilton, or a strong barley wine, like Young's Old Nick, Thomas Hardy's Ale and J W Lees Vintage Harvest Ale. Having said that, Colston Bassett Stilton with Sam Adams Triple Bock, a combination I enjoyed at an American craft brewers' dinner, is one of my all-time favourite pairings.

* Ultra-creamy cheeses
If they're savoury, like Explorateur, we'd go for a Belgian tripel. With a sweet cheese, like mascarpone, you could drink a fruit beer or a coffee or chocolate beer, which would give a similar effect to a tiramisu.

* Cheeseboards
If you're serving several cheeses at once, particularly artisanal cheeses, you need a beer that can cope with the strongest cheese on the board – that's usually a washed-rind cheese or a blue. This suggests a strong beer with a touch of sweetness: strong abbey ales, like Maredsous 8 and Chimay Grande Reserve, saison or saison-style beers and the barley wines detailed under Blue cheeses. Less sweet, rich British ales can struggle – we'd go for something really powerful, like Batemans XXXB or the repulsively named but eminently drinkable Skullsplitter.

Warm cheesy things...

If there's one thing even better than bread and cheese, it's bread – or toast – and warm, molten cheese. You can use beer to create the desired gooey consistency, as in the fondue below or the Welsh rabbit leeks on page 130, or simply create a toasted cheese snack to accompany your favourite brew.

Beer & cheese fondue
If you're making a dish as simple as fondue, you need top-quality cheese. I like to use a blend that includes Gruyère or Comté.

serves 2

about 425g finely sliced or coarsely grated cheese,
   with rinds removed: say 150g Cheddar,
   150g cave-aged Gruyère or Comté, and
   125g vintage Gouda
2 tsp potato flour or cornflour
1 clove of garlic, halved
175ml strong blonde or amber ale
1–2 tbsp not-too peaty whisky (optional)
freshly ground black pepper
sourdough, pain de campagne or ciabatta, to serve
You will need a cast iron fondue pan and burner

Toss the sliced or grated cheese with the potato flour or cornflour. Leave until it comes to room temperature. Rub the inside of the pan with the cut garlic.

Start off the fondue on your cooker. Pour in the beer and heat until almost boiling. Add a good handful of grated cheese and stir until it melts, moving it about in the pan with a zig-zag motion. (Stirring it round and round as you do for a sauce makes the cheese more likely to separate from the liquid.)

Gradually add the remaining cheese until you have a smooth, thick mass (this takes about 10 minutes, less with practice). If it seems too thick, add a little hot water. Add the whisky, if using, and season with freshly ground black pepper.

Place over your fondue burner and serve with small, bite-sized chunks of sourdough or country bread. Use long fondue forks to dip the bread into the fondue, stirring to prevent the fondue solidifying.

Best beer match This is a seriously rich dish, so you don't need to gild the lily with a very strong beer. We think that an amber or a dark lager is the best match.

Gorgonzola & pear bruschetta

This incredibly easy dish is what became known a couple of years ago as a cheesert – a combination of a cheese course and a dessert. You could double or treble up the recipe and serve it as a starter with a lightly dressed mixed leaf salad with a few walnuts.

serves 1

1 thin to medium slice of sourdough bread

1 ripe Conference pear

1 tbsp light olive oil or sunflower oil

½ tsp sugar

50g mild Gorgonzola or Dolcelatte

2 tbsp double cream

freshly ground black pepper

a few snipped chives

watercress or wild rocket, to garnish

Lightly toast the bread. Quarter, peel and core the pear. Heat a frying pan, then add the oil. Let it heat for a minute, then tip in the sliced pear. Stir-fry it for a minute, then add the sugar and fry until lightly caramelized. Put the pear slices on top of the toast.

Leaving the pan off the heat, add the diced Gorgonzola or Dolcelatte and 2 tbsp of cream, and melt in the residual heat of the pan. Season with black pepper and pour over the pear slices.

Sprinkle with a few snipped chives, and garnish with watercress or wild rocket.

Best beer match This is great with a strong, rich Belgian beer, like Leffe Radieuse, or with a saison-style beer.

" With a Monty-Pythonesque name like Silly for one of its leading brands, it's hard to take the saison style seriously, but if you're a lover of rich, fruity, full-flavoured beers, do track them down. They are a speciality of the south of Belgium and were originally brewed in the spring to be drunk in the summer. Like IPAs, they pick up well on spices and are also great with roast pork. "

sweet treats

The most surprising part of the whole voyage of exploration that this book has represented is the discovery of just how wonderful beers are with – and in – desserts and cakes. Of course, I'd tasted the odd combination, most notably porter and chocolate, and raspberry beer with cheesecake, but had regarded them as exceptions that proved the general rule that dry drinks don't work with sweet foods.

In fact, the reverse seems to be the case with beer. Although a dry drink, it tempers and balances the sweetness of many desserts. The at-first curious combination of a creamy dessert, like a crème brûlée or a tiramisu, with a stout has a similar effect to a black coffee: a welcome note of bitterness that stops the cream being cloying. Sharp fruit beers have a similar effect, bringing fresh fruit flavours into the equation, picking up on fruits that are already on the plate.

Of course, the beer world has its own equivalent of sweet wines: barley wines, such as J W Lees Vintage Harvest Ale and Thomas Hardy's Ale, are brilliant with the kind of dessert (especially fruit cakes and Christmas pudding) that you'd drink with a liqueur muscat or a port.

You can also use beer undiluted in a dessert, as I've done to dramatic effect with the sorbets and jellies on pages 158–61. These are real show-stoppers at the end of a meal, guaranteed to convert guests who don't think of themselves as beer lovers.

You can also achieve a striking contrast to a dessert with a beer to finish a meal on a high note. Stout, in particular, plays this role to perfection, not only for its coffee-ish flavour but for its dramatic black colour. I really like the combination of a chocolate stout with the Banana tatin on page 146 – more so, I confess, than the usual pairing of chocolate stout and a chocolate dessert. (Think chocolate and banana... mmmm.)

The one note that doesn't work too well with sweet flavours is hop bitterness, so it's best to avoid hoppy ales with desserts.

Banana tatin

Bananas and chocolate stout are one of the best beer and food combinations in my view. Better even than chocolate and porter! A tatin, once you get the hang of it, is not difficult, particularly if you use the technique of making the caramel in the pan, which I picked up from Gordon Ramsay's *Just Desserts* (Quadrille, 2001). Your bananas should be just underripe – not green, but not bright yellow either.

serves 4–6

250g ready-made puff pastry *
75g good-quality butter at room temperature
75g caster sugar
1 tbsp lemon juice
4–6 firm, but not underripe, bananas (about 750g in total)
You will need a medium-sized (23cm) frying pan or
   tatin dish with an ovenproof handle

Roll out the pastry, invert a large dinner plate over the top and cut round the edge to give you a large circle about 26cm in diameter. Prick the pastry lightly all over, place back on the plate and transfer to the fridge.

Spread the butter thickly over the base of the pan and halfway up the sides. Shake the sugar evenly over the butter and sprinkle with the lemon juice. Peel and cut all but 2 of the bananas into 3cm lengths and stack them upright over the base of the pan, packing them in closely. Cut the remaining bananas in half vertically to go round the edges.

Preheat the oven to 200°C/400°F/Gas 6. Put the pan over a medium heat and leave for about 15 minutes, shaking the pan occasionally. The butter will first melt, then gradually form a caramel with the sugar.

Take the pan off the heat once the mixture begins to turn golden brown. Leave the pan for 5 minutes for the bubbling to subside, then carefully lower the pastry onto the pan, tucking the edges down the sides. (Don't worry about the excess pastry – it will shrink slightly when cooked.)

Put the pan in the oven and bake for 15 minutes, then turn the heat down to 180°C/350°F/Gas 4 and cook for another 10–15 minutes until the pastry is crisp and golden.

Remove the pan from the oven and leave for 10 minutes, work round the edge of the tart with a knife, then carefully invert it onto a large plate. If you find a few pieces of banana have stuck to the base of the pan, simply prise them off with a round-bladed knife and stick them back on top of the tart, caramelized-side upwards. Serve the tart warm with vanilla ice cream or whipped double cream.

* It's frankly easier to use ready-made puff pastry, which usually comes in packs of 375g. Ready-rolled pastry often comes as a rectangle, rather than a circle, so you'll still need to roll it out a bit.

Best beer match This is a great partner for a chocolate- or coffee-flavoured beer (the Meantime Brewing Company make fantastic ones in great bottles) or a mellow porter.

" Coffee beer may sound totally weird if you haven't tried it, but if you like the hit of a strong espresso, you'll love it. The coffee beer made by Meantime has impeccable credentials – it's produced mainly from Fairtrade Araba Bourbon beans from Rwanda's Abahuzamugambi Ba Kawa Co-operative and roasted by one of London's best coffee suppliers, Union Coffee Roasters. Coffee beer is also very good with dark chocolate... "

Baked apples with winter ale

Apple-based desserts are one of the best pairings with sweet wines, so how do they fare with beer? Very well, particularly if they take the form of a pie, cobbler or crumble (pastry is always good with beer) or if they're caramelized, as in a tatin, or baked with dried fruits, as here. A spicy winter ale makes the most fabulous rich sugary juices to go with a baked apple. However, this does tend to make any beer you drink with it taste quite bitter, so you'd be better off with a barley wine – that's if you want a beer to accompany it at all.

serves 4

4 medium to large Bramley apples
40–50g raisins
40g soft brown sugar mixed with ½ tsp cinnamon
  or mixed spice
25g butter + extra for greasing the dish
100ml winter ale, such as Duchy Originals Winter Ale

Preheat the oven to 200º/400ºF/Gas 6.

Place each apple on a chopping board stalk-side up. Using a sharp knife, cut a square round the core, right through the apple and lift out the core. (You can obviously do this more easily with an apple corer.) Score round the circumference of the apple so that you cut through the skin but not into the fruit.

Place the apples in a lightly buttered baking dish. Stuff a little sugar down the holes you've made, then add the raisins and the rest of the sugar. Push a good lump of butter into the top of each apple.

Pour 3–4 tbsp of water around the apples to stop the juices burning, and bake for 20 minutes.

Turn the oven down to 190ºC/375ºF/Gas 5, pour in the beer and return the dish to the oven for another 10–15 minutes, depending on the size of the apples. Serve with cream, vanilla ice cream or custard.

Best beer match Keen though we are to drink beer at every possible opportunity, we're not sure that you need one here.

Teabreads & cakes

At Christmas, I normally stick to tried-and-tested family recipes, but last year, in the interests of researching this book, I included beer in both my Christmas pudding and Christmas cake. The results were brilliant, so much so that I'll be making them again this year. Try the supercharged barm brack, too!

Barm brack

(Illustrated left) An adaptation of a classic Irish teabread made with Manns Brown Ale and dark sugar which gives it a particularly rich, fudgy quality. Unbelievably easy.

serves 8–10

175ml cold tea *

150ml Manns Brown Ale

150g dark muscovado sugar

350g mixed dried fruit

1 large free-range egg, lightly beaten

275g self-raising flour

1/2 tsp mixed spice

You will need a well-greased 900g loaf tin, lined with
   baking parchment

Pour the tea and ale into a large bowl, stir in the sugar, then add the fruit and leave in the fridge overnight.

When ready to cook, preheat the oven to 180°C/ 350°F/Gas 4. Add the beaten egg to the soaked fruit, sift in the self-raising flour and mixed spice, and mix thoroughly.

Tip the mixture into a well-greased, lined loaf tin and bake for 1 1/2 hours, turning the heat down to 170°C/325°F/Gas 3 halfway through the cooking time. Leave in the tin for 10 minutes, then turn out and cool on a wire rack. Wrap in foil and leave until the following day.

Serve sliced with butter.

* Best to use a classic builders' tea for this, rather than anything fancy. Brew it strong but don't let it stew.

Dark, sticky Christmas cake with prunes & Guinness

This is based on a recipe from Dan Lepard, which was published in the *Guardian*, but I've fiddled around with it here and there. Do use organic dried fruit in it – you'll get a much better result.

serves 10–12

250g currants

150g *mi-cuit* (semi-soft) prunes, preferably
   from Agen, cut into small pieces

200g organic dried apricots, cut into small
   pieces

125g large raisins

grated rind of 1 unwaxed orange

150ml Guinness or similar stout

200g unsalted butter

1 tbsp mixed spice

150ml treacle

200g dark muscovado sugar

2 large eggs, lightly beaten

300g spelt or wholemeal flour

1 tsp baking powder

You will need a deep, loose-bottomed cake tin,
   about 20cm in diameter, double-lined with
   baking parchment

Preheat the oven to 170°C/325°F/Gas 3.

Combine the dried fruit and orange rind in a bowl. Pour the Guinness or stout into a saucepan, heat gently until hot (but not boiling) and pour over the fruit. Heat the butter in a saucepan over a gentle heat, and skim off the milky curds that rise to the surface.

Simmer until it begins to deepen in colour, then stir in the mixed spice and treacle. Add to the fruit, along with the sugar, and stir well.

Cool the mixture, then gradually add the lightly beaten eggs. Sift the flour with the baking powder and add to the mixture. Spoon the mixture into the lined tin, pressing it down well and smoothing the surface.

Bake in the preheated oven for an hour, covering the top of the cake with foil if it starts to brown too quickly, then turn the heat down to 140°C/275°F/ Gas 1 for a further 1 1/2–2 hours until a skewer inserted in the cake comes out clean.

Remove the cake from the oven and cool in the tin. Peel off the the baking parchment, cover with fresh parchment, then wrap tightly in foil. It will keep well for up to a month.

Desserts with fruit beers

Once I got on a roll with fruit beers, I had trouble stopping them taking over this entire chapter. They were divine with cheesecake, sublime with Bakewell tart, wicked with chocolate and cherry roulade. They're also brilliant with pancakes and fritters, and jellies and sorbets.

Apricot pancakes

Pancakes, sweet or savoury, are a particularly good match for beer, but I'm not convinced about the virtue of putting beer in them (unlike batters or doughs where you want a good rise). Although apricots are obviously at their best in the summer when they're in season in Europe, you can find them during the winter as well. They tend to be unripe then, though, which is where the apricot brandy in this recipe comes in handy.

serves 3–4

for the pancakes:

110g plain flour

¼ tsp salt

2 large fresh free-range eggs

275ml semi-skimmed milk

25g cooled melted butter + another 25g butter for greasing the pan and brushing the pancakes

icing sugar, to serve

for the apricot filling:

500g fresh apricots

3 heaped tbsp soft-set apricot jam, preferably unsweetened

4 tbsp apricot brandy + extra to serve

lemon juice, to taste (optional)

You will need a medium-sized pancake pan

First, make the batter. Mix the flour and salt in a large bowl. Make a hollow in the centre. Beat the eggs lightly with the milk, then add 25g cooled melted butter. Gradually pour into the flour, stirring all the time, and beat well with a wooden spoon. (Alternatively, make the batter in a food processor or blender.) Set the batter aside for half an hour while you make the filling.

Halve and stone the apricots and cut into small chunks. Put in a saucepan with the apricot jam and apricot brandy, cover with a lid and cook until the apricots are soft but still holding their shape. Check for sweetness, adding a little lemon juice if you want them sharper or a splash more apricot brandy if they need sweetening, and set aside.

Beat the pancake batter again. Heat a pancake pan until hot, add a small chunk of butter and rub it round the pan with some scrunched-up kitchen towel. Scoop out a small cup or ladleful of batter and tip it into the pan, swirling it round quickly so the whole base of the pan is covered with batter.

Cook for about 30 seconds until the edges begin to brown, then flip over with a spatula and cook the other side. Stack the pancakes on a plate as you make them, interleaved with sheets of greaseproof paper so they don't stick.

Heat the oven to 190°C/375°F/Gas 5. Butter a shallow ovenproof dish. Fill each pancake with a tablespoon of the apricot filling and roll up or fold into four. Arrange the filled pancakes in the dish and brush with the remaining melted butter. Bake for 10–15 minutes until the pancakes are hot through and crisp on the top. Sift over a little icing sugar.

Serve the pancakes with an extra splash of apricot brandy and a scoop of vanilla ice cream.

Best beer match An apricot- or peach-flavoured beer would be lovely with this.

Quick fruit fritters
The easiest pud imaginable. I like to make these fritters with a selection of different fruits, rather than just the usual apple and banana. Fresh pineapple, apricots and plums are good, especially if they're slightly tart, rather than overripe. And use a bog-standard lager – you don't need a hoppy flavour.

serves 4

a selection of fruit, such as a Granny Smith apple,
  a banana, a couple of stoned apricots or plums
  or a few chunks of fresh pineapple
2 tbsp caster sugar
¼ tsp ground cinnamon
fresh vegetable or sunflower oil for frying
icing sugar, to serve

for the batter:

100g self-raising flour
a small pinch of salt
chilled lager, to mix
1 medium egg white

Peel, core and stone the fruit, as appropriate, and cut into even-sized pieces. Put the sugar in a bowl, mix in the cinnamon, add the fruit pieces and toss together.

Put the flour in a bowl with the salt, and mix in just enough lager to make a very thick batter. Beat vigorously with a wire whisk or a wooden spoon. Beat the egg white until stiff and fold it into the batter. Put a wok on a burner, fill it about a quarter full with fresh oil and heat for 2–3 minutes until the oil is hot.

Drop a few of the fruit pieces into the batter, make sure they're thoroughly coated, then, using a large spoon, drop them into the hot oil a few at a time. As soon as you can see the underside of the fritter is brown (about 30 seconds), flip it over and cook the other side.

Remove the fritters with a slotted spoon and put them on a plate lined with kitchen towel. Repeat with the remaining fruit and eat immediately, sifting over a little icing sugar as you serve them. It's worth handing the fritters round as they're ready as they taste best when they're really hot. They're very good with vanilla ice cream.

Best beer match **These would go well with a chilled peach, mango or passion fruit beer.**

Bakewell tart

It stands to reason that raspberry-flavoured beer should go with a dessert made with almonds and raspberries. But just how well you wouldn't believe.

serves 6

110g unsalted butter
3 large free-range eggs
110g caster sugar
100g ground almonds
2 level tbsp plain flour, sifted
1 level tsp almond essence
6–7 tbsp soft-set raspberry jam
225g fresh raspberries
25g flaked almonds

for the pastry:

250g plain flour
2 tbsp icing sugar
125g chilled butter
1 large egg yolk (+ the white, lightly beaten)
a pinch of salt
You will need a deep flan tin 23–25cm wide

First, make the pastry. Sift the flour and icing sugar into a large bowl. Cut the butter into small cubes, cut the butter into the flour, then rub lightly with your fingertips until the mixture is the consistency of coarse breadcrumbs.

Mix the egg yolk with 2 tbsp ice-cold water, add to the pastry mix, mix lightly and pull together into a ball, adding extra water if needed. Shape into a flat disc and refrigerate for at least half an hour. (You can also, of course, make this in a food processor.)

Roll out the pastry into a circle large enough to fit the tin with a bit of overlap. Carefully lower the pastry into the tin, pressing it lightly into the sides and cut off the excess pastry round the edges. Prick the base lightly and chill the pastry case for 10–15 minutes while you preheat the oven to 200°C/400°F/Gas 6.

Line the pastry case with foil and bake for 10–12 minutes, then remove the foil and brush the base of the pastry case with the reserved egg white. Return to the oven for another 3–4 minutes, then set aside for a couple of minutes while you make the filling.

Slowly melt the butter in a small saucepan. Whisk or beat the eggs with the sugar until light and frothy, then add the ground almonds, sifted flour, almond essence and melted butter. Spoon the jam onto the base of the tart and spread evenly.

Scatter over the raspberries in an even layer, then pour over the topping. Bake at 190ºC/375ºF/Gas 5 for about 40 minutes until risen and nicely browned, scattering the almonds over the surface 5 minutes before the end of the cooking time. Serve warm with double cream.

Best beer match Our dream beer with this would be New Glarus Raspberry Tart from Wisconsin, but any raspberry beer would do nicely.

Summer berry cheesecake

One of my most popular recipes ever – and made to go with a fruit beer.

serves 6–8

for the crust:

110g digestive biscuits

50g butter

for the first layer:

2 x 200g packs Philadelphia cream cheese *

2 large eggs

100g caster sugar

¼ tsp Madagascar vanilla extract or
  vanilla essence

for the second layer:

284ml carton soured cream

150 ml Greek-style yoghurt

2½ tbsp caster sugar

1 tsp vanilla extract or vanilla essence

for the berry topping:

3 tbsp redcurrant jelly

2 tsp arrowroot

125g fresh raspberries

75g redcurrants, de-stalked

50g blueberries

You will need a 21cm loose-based or
  spring-release cake tin

Preheat the oven to 190ºC/375ºF/Gas 5.

Crush the digestive biscuits (the easiest way to do this is to put them in a strong plastic bag, seal it and thump them with a rolling pin). Gently melt the butter in a saucepan, cool slightly and add the crushed biscuits. Press evenly into the base of the cake tin.

Mix the Philadelphia cream cheese, eggs, sugar and vanilla extract together thoroughly – a doddle in a food processor. If you do it by hand, add the eggs, one by one. Pour over the biscuit base, smooth the top and bake in the oven for 20 minutes or until just set. Set aside for 20 minutes to firm up.

Mix the soured cream with the yoghurt, sugar and vanilla essence and spoon evenly over the first layer. Return to the oven for 10 minutes, then take out and cool.

Refrigerate for at least 6 hours or overnight. About an hour before serving, put the redcurrant jelly into a small pan and heat gently until almost boiling. Mix the arrowroot with 1 tbsp water and tip into the jelly. Stir until the jelly is clear and thick, then take off the heat, tip in the berries, mix lightly and cool. Ease a knife down the sides of the cake tin, then release the clamp or push up the base. Spoon the berries evenly over the cheesecake and return to the fridge until ready to serve.

* It's important to use Philadelphia cream cheese because it has the right texture for this recipe.

Best beer match Easy: a raspberry- or cherry-flavoured beer.

Chocolate & cherry roulade

This spectacular-looking dessert might sound daunting to make but it's actually no more difficult than a chocolate mousse, provided that you have the right kit (see below).

serves 6

for the roulade:

175g Belgian dark luxury chocolate *

2 tbsp stout, porter or black coffee

5 large eggs, separated

125g caster sugar

for the filling:

350g pitted morello cherries (Polish ones are best) or stoned fresh, black cherries

2 tbsp kriek

1 tbsp kirsch (optional)

284ml carton double cream

1–2 tbsp caster sugar, to taste

to assemble:

icing sugar

You will need a 33 x 23cm shallow rectangular Swiss-roll tin, some non-stick baking parchment, several large bowls and an electric hand whisk

Preheat the oven to 190°C/375°F/Gas 5. Lightly grease the baking tin and line with a piece of non-stick baking parchment. Break up the chocolate and put it in a bowl with the stout, porter or coffee.

Set the bowl over a pan of simmering water, making sure the base of the pan doesn't touch the water. Leave to melt, stir once to amalgamate and take off the heat. Put the eggs and sugar in another bowl and whisk together for a couple of minutes until light and moussey. Fold in the chocolate mixture with a large spoon. In another bowl – and with a clean whisk – whisk the egg whites until they just hold their shape. Add a couple of tablespoons of the egg whites to the chocolate mixture to lighten it, then fold in the rest of the egg whites lightly without overmixing.

Tip the chocolate mixture gently into the baking tin, and lightly and evenly spread it over the base of the tin. Bake in the preheated oven for 15–20 minutes until the top is risen and firm to the touch. Leave the roulade in the tin, cover with another sheet of baking parchment and lay a damp tea towel over the top. Leave for at least 3 hours.

Meanwhile, drain the cherries, if bottled, or stone them, if fresh, halving or quartering them if they're particularly large. Put them in a bowl, with the kriek and a few drops of kirsch, and refrigerate.

To assemble the roulade, lay a large piece of baking parchment on your work surface and dust it with sifted icing sugar. Carefully tip the roulade onto the paper. Peel away the baking parchment off the base of the roulade and trim the edges. Strain the cherries, reserving the juice. Lightly whip the cream until just holding its shape, fold in the cherry juice and sweeten to taste.

Spread the cream over the roulade, leaving a space round the edges and scatter the cherries on top. Using the baking parchment, roll the roulade up like a swiss roll and carefully transfer to a serving plate. Sift over a little extra icing sugar.

* You need chocolate that isn't too high in cocoa, otherwise the chocolate may 'seize' and go solid. Choose one with about 55–60% cocoa solids (available in the baking section of supermarkets).

Best beer match Liefmans Kriek or other cherry beers.

Beer sorbets

Weissbiers, witbiers and fruit beers make sensational sorbets, but if you're to preserve their unique character, they need careful handling – you're freezing a mix that contains a fair amount of alcohol and sugar, which is not going to freeze as hard as a conventional ice cream. If you use less beer and more fruit juice or purée, you'll lose that delicious sour fruit flavour.

So, freeze the container you're going to spoon the mix into and the glasses you serve it in. You'll also get a better result with a sorbetière or ice cream maker. They're not expensive, and you can keep the bowl in the freezer for whenever you want to run up a quick and impressive dessert!

Weissbier sorbet
I tasted a sorbet like this at a fabulous beer dinner at a brilliant restaurant called Fingerprint in Hersching, just outside Munich. You get all the aromatic character of the beer, which makes it a brilliantly impressive palate cleanser or a refreshing end to a spicy meal. The quantities I've given for the sugar syrup will make enough for two batches of sorbet. You can keep the leftover syrup in a sealed container or jar for a couple of weeks in the fridge.

serves 6 as a palate cleanser, 4 as a dessert

250g caster sugar
3 tbsp liquid glucose
330ml bottle of weissbier or witbier

If you're using an ice cream maker, put the bowl in the freezer for the time recommended by the manufacturer (usually at least 18 hours). Put the sugar in a saucepan with the liquid glucose. Add 200ml of water and place the pan over a very low heat until the sugar has completely dissolved, stirring occasionally. Bring to the boil without stirring and boil hard for 3 minutes, again without stirring. Take off the heat, cool and refrigerate. Put the beer in the fridge, too.

When the beer and syrup are both chilled, pour the beer into a measuring jug and add syrup up to the 450ml mark. Mix well. Pour the mixture into an ice cream machine and churn until frozen. Scoop into a lidded plastic container, put the lid on and freeze for at least two hours until firm. (The level of alcohol means that it won't go completely hard.)

Serve on its own as a palate cleanser, with other sorbets or with exotic fruits.

* If you don't have an ice cream maker, you can freeze the base mixture and whizz it 3 or 4 times in a food processor during the freezing process instead. However, you won't get as much volume or such a smooth result.

Cherry beer sorbet
(*Illustrated left*) Again, the sugar syrup will make enough for two sorbets.

175g caster sugar
2 tbsp liquid glucose
375ml bottle kriek (Belle-Vue Kriek has a good
  colour for this sorbet)
4 tbsp juice from a jar of Polish morello cherries

To make the sugar syrup, follow the instructions given above for the Weissbier sorbet, and chill both the syrup and the beer.

Pour the beer into a measuring jug, then spoon out 4 tbsp of beer and replace with the cherry juice. Pour in sugar syrup up to the 450ml mark and mix.

Pour the mixture into an ice cream maker and churn until frozen. Scoop into a lidded plastic container, put the lid on and freeze for at least 2 hours until firm. Serve on its own as a palate cleanser, with other sorbets or with fresh berry fruits.

* See above if you don't have an ice cream maker.

Beer jellies *(Illustrated overleaf)*

These jellies are deliberately left less sweet than most commercial jellies so that the flavour of the beer comes through. I find them really refreshing but you can, of course, add extra sugar if you want.

Raspberry & cherry beer jellies

serves 4

4 small sheets of gelatine (about 6g or ¼ of
 a 25g pack)
375ml kriek or other cherry- or raspberry-flavoured beer
470g jar of pitted morello cherries (Polish ones are best)
2–3 tbsp sugar syrup or caster sugar
125g fresh or frozen raspberries

Place the gelatine in a bowl of cold water and leave to soak for 3 minutes until soft. Measure the kriek into a jug and top up to the 400ml mark with syrup from the cherries. Pour into a saucepan and add the sugar. Put over a very low heat until the sugar has dissolved, then heat until lukewarm (it shouldn't boil).

Squeeze the soaked gelatine leaves, add them to the beer mixture and stir to dissolve, then set aside to cool. Drain the remaining syrup from the cherries and rinse the raspberries. Put an assortment of berries in the bottom of four glasses or glass dishes, then pour over enough jelly to cover them.

Put the glasses in the fridge to chill. As soon as the jelly in the glasses has set (about 1 hour), add another layer of fruit and jelly. Repeat until the fruit and jelly are used up, ending with a layer of jelly.

Leave in the fridge to set for another 45 minutes to 1 hour before serving with lightly whipped cream, sweetened with a little vanilla sugar or vanilla ice cream.

Mango & passion fruit beer jellies   Follow the above recipe, substituting passion fruit beer for the kriek (top up with tropical fruit juice, passion fruit or mango juice to make it up to the 400ml mark of the measuring jug), then gradually mix in about 400g of cubed mango and passion fruit pulp and liquid jelly, as described above. Adjust sweetness to taste (you can always add a squeeze of lemon juice if it's too sweet).

Blueberry & peach beer jellies   Follow the above recipe, substituting peach-flavoured beer for the kriek (top up with white cranberry and grape juice to make it up to the 400ml mark of the measuring jug), then gradually mix in about 400g of cubed peach or nectarine and blueberries and liquid jelly, as described above. Adjust sweetness to taste, as above.

" Cherry and raspberry beers have traditionally been a Belgian speciality. In general, they're based on lambic (wild yeast-fermented) beers, although Liefmans famous Kriek is based on a brown ale. The long infusion of fruit produces a wonderful balance of sweet and sour, which surprisingly goes equally well with sweet and savoury dishes. "

From left to right:
Mango & passion fruit beer jelly,
raspberry & cherry beer jelly and
blueberry & peach beer jelly.

entertaining
with beer

Hands up who drinks beer when they're on their own but serves wine when their friends come round or on special occasions? Don't be embarrassed – we've all done it. To put the best possible construction on it, we can say it's because we want our friends to feel comfortable with the sort of drinks we're offering them but we don't tend to make those kind of allowances with food. We serve the kind of food we like or feel comfortable and confident cooking.

The reality is that many beer lovers feel a bit tentative about serving beer, as if it's not somehow as serious a drink as wine. But if you've read through this book, you will have seen how far that is from being the case. Serving craft beers with your food is, in fact, treating your friends to the best the beer world has to offer, something few of us can afford to do with wine. It's on a par with serving the best grass-fed beef, the freshest vegetables and fruits, the best artisanal cheeses.

You don't, of course, have to construct the entire meal around beer. As a wine lover, too, I'm perfectly happy to switch to beer with dessert or with cheese, a good way to entice your wine-drinking friends into beer-drinking habits. (We don't buy into the old chestnut about not mixing grape and grain by the way. It's the overall amount of alcohol you consume that has the hangover-inducing potential, not the type of alcohol you drink.)

Serve beer when you might be expected to serve it but offer a more interesting beer than your friends will anticipate. An IPA instead of a lager with a curry, a witbier or bière blanche with a Thai meal, some good golden or amber lagers with a barbecue. There are a number of companies now who offer small quantities of cask-conditioned ale online, such as www.cellarmandirect.com (see page 182).

You can also buy large, 70cl bottles, which makes a statement of intent that the beer is for sharing, not just for the dedicated hopheads in the party. Start by putting beer as well as wine on the table when you have a Sunday roast or serve a robust beef stew or steak and ale pie. Then do the same next time you have a dinner party.

You'll win your friends round, we promise.

How to plan a beer dinner (or lunch)

Those of you who have been to beer dinners will know they tend to be ambitious six- or seven-course affairs, designed to showcase as many different styles of beer as possible. They're fascinating experiences but best left to professional kitchens, we feel.

That doesn't mean you can't make quite a show if you decide to serve a beer dinner (or lunch) at home. Our philosophy is if you choose your ales with care, then it doesn't matter whether you cook one dish or three. You can buy the rest in and your guests will still be impressed.

The very phrase 'beer dinner' suggests that the starting point is going to be the beer rather than the food, though you can play it either way. You might invite some friends round to taste different examples of a particular beer style, like Pilseners, wheat beers or amber ales, then serve some food afterwards that matches them well (this could simply be snacks, not a full meal – a selection of different cheeses or a smorgasbord, for example).

You could have a meal that was exclusively paired with beers from one country, with Belgium, Germany or the US being obvious options, although a Scottish beer-partnered Burns Night dinner, based on British regional specialities partnered with beers from the same part of the country, might be fun. On the other hand, you could use one of the recipes in this book as a starting point – the Fabada (see page 103), for example – and build a meal round that. There are some ideas to start you thinking on the page opposite.

Whichever approach you take, try to balance the beers you serve so that you progress from lighter beers to those that are more intense in flavour. So, if you start with a stout, as you might for a St Patrick's Day supper, you'll need to carry on in robust vein, possibly with another type of stout or porter or a full-bodied characterful ale.

It's fair to say that this sort of evening works better with consenting adults who are serious about their beer and as interested as you in comparing different brews and how they react with food. If you're throwing a party or a large barbecue, it's better to keep the beer options rather more straightforward, as people will almost certainly quaff rather than sip.

Some ideas for beer menus

A Spanish evening for 6–8

Kick off with some shop-bought tapas which you could serve with a light Spanish lager or Pilsener. Make the Fabada (page 103) the centrepiece of the meal, offering a Spanish beer like Alhambra 1925 or a Basque beer like L'Amalthée, and finish with a bought-in crema catalana or crème caramel.

A slap-up dinner party for 6

Offer some smoked salmon nibbles and a glass of Deus. Move on to Steak with Innis & Gunn (page 86), trebling the quantities, and serve with the same beer or a strong, dark Trappist ale. Next, serve the Chocolate & cherry roulade (page 156) with a kriek, then finish off with a cheeseboard and a barley wine, like J W Lees Vintage Harvest Ale. You could also serve a Meantime Coffee Beer and chocolates.

A simple Saturday night supper for 4

Start with the French-style chicken liver pâté with cognac (page 27) or a bought-in pâté served with an American IPA or a Belgian tripel ale. Then serve the Sierra Nevada chicken (page 75) with a Sierra Nevada Pale Ale, and finish up with a Bakewell tart (page 154) served with a framboise or other raspberry beer.

Sunday lunch with a twist

Make the Roast pork belly with black pudding & potato & apple purée (page 84) the centrepiece of the meal.

It's particularly good with beer, so take a look at the suggestions given with the recipe. Make life simple for yourself by simply serving some nuts and nibbles like Paul's cracking cheese straws first (page 20) with a best bitter, then finish up with a Banana tatin (page 146) with a chocolate or coffee stout.

A Belgian beer dinner

Again, pâté would be a good way to start, served with a strong golden ale like Duvel. Then you could either serve a Carbonnade of beef with Orval (page 91) or Pot roast pheasant with bacon, onion & apple & spiced juniper cabbage (page 80) with an oude gueuze. You could then serve a Trappist cheese with a Trappist beer like Chimay Bleu, and finish with a Cherry beer sorbet (page 159).

A Greek(ish) veggie supper

Serve a selection of meze such as hummus and olives, including the (admittedly not very Greek but it does go well) Beetroot & cream cheese spread (page 23), accompanied by a light Pilsener. The main course could be the Mushroom moussaka (page 133), served with a dunkel or dubbel beer, then you could finish up with some grilled or roasted peaches served with Greek yoghurt, pine nuts and a drizzle of honey and a peach-flavoured beer.

See also the seasonal menu ideas given overleaf.

" The glasses you serve your beer in make a big difference to the way your beer looks and tastes. Sure, few of us have the cupboard space to run to the 100-odd different glasses the Belgians have to match their beers, but don't hesitate to pour a wheat beer or a fruit beer into a champagne glass or a full-bodied ale into a red wine goblet rather than into a pint glass (fine in a pub, not so good for the dinner table). Even better, treat yourself – or get someone to treat you – to a few designer beer glasses, like those made by Dartington in Devon. "

A beer for all seasons

The idea of seasonality is firmly entrenched in beer culture, with many breweries producing a range of seasonal ales or beers that are brewed for release at a particular time of year, such as doppelbocks for the spring and Märzen for the Oktoberfest. Drinking seasonally also makes sense if you want to show off seasonal ingredients and dishes at their best, creating a dining experience that's satisfying at every level.

Spring

With temperatures climbing, it's time to enjoy the first of the season's new vegetables and herbs – asparagus, peas and broad beans, and the first salad leaves. It's also time to enjoy light seafood like crab, scallops and salmon, and chicken.

Beers to enjoy Witbiers/bières blanches and similar cloudy wheat beers; light Pilseners and lagers; pale ales and bocks, if you like to follow the German tradition.

Recipes to try Spicy crab crostini (page 54); Crab, prawn & dill fishcakes (page 55); Prawn, fennel & leek risotto (page 47); Sierra Nevada chicken (page 75).

Summer

Summer is a time for outdoor eating, for pub lunches and picnics, for pool parties and barbecues. Food can swing from simple salads to the kaleidoscope of flavours you get with a plate of barbecued meats and salads. Vegetables are Mediterranean, bright, bold in flavour, while summer fruits are a treat you must make sure you enjoy.

Beers to enjoy English bitters and IPAs; blonde, golden and amber ales; summer ales; honey beers; cherry and raspberry fruit beers.

Recipes to try Ham & parsley pâté (page 27); Chicken Caesar salad (page 76); Emmental, fennel & apple salad with honey, mustard & yoghurt dressing (page 124); My perfect ploughman's (page 138); Summer berry cheesecake (page 155); Raspberry & cherry beer jellies (page 160); Cherry beer sorbet (page 159).

For barbecues Beer-can chicken (page 72); Salmon burgers with goats' cheese & sun-dried tomatoes (page 57); Sticky barbecued ribs (page 88).

Autumn

As the nights draw in, flavours deepen, becoming richer and more earthy. This is the season for squash and pumpkin, mushrooms and game, apples and stone fruits. There are plenty of excuses for a celebration – a harvest supper, your own Oktoberfest, Hallowe'en and Bonfire Night. As the weather gets colder, the dishes become more robust still, autumn edging into winter stews, casseroles and pies.

Beers to enjoy Hearty British ales, amber ales and lagers; Belgian tripels; brown ales and pumpkin ales; dark Belgian Trappist ales; bières de garde; the funky flavours of an oude gueuze.

Recipes to try Mushroom & mustard soup (page 18); Roast butternut squash, chestnut & wild mushroom fusilli (page 44); Sausages & stoemp (page 100); Shearers' stew (page 90); Roast pork belly with black pudding & potato & apple purée (page 84); Pot roast pheasant with bacon, onion & apple & spiced juniper cabbage (page 80).

For an Oktoberfest celebration Cold meats and Bavarian potato salad (page 127); Oktoberfest chicken (page 68), Weissbier sorbet (page 159).

Winter
Substantial cold-weather comfort food makes up for the freezing temperatures. This is the time for chunky soups, stews and casseroles, for pot roasts and pies, for using beer in, as well as drinking with, your favourite dishes. The time of year when you need a nibble of cheese and a nightcap to send you off to bed.

Beers to enjoy Seasonal winter brews; British ales and porters; strong dark Trappist beers and bières de garde; doppelbocks; Scottish ales and warm, sweet barley wines.

Beer for Christmas Christmas can be celebrated just as well with beer as with wine. Kick off with a glass of strong golden ale or an IPA, a beer that will also carry you through the turkey, although you could switch to an amber, a saison or even a pumpkin ale. With Christmas pud, you could drink a Christmas pudding ale, though

you may have used a similar beer in it. We'd be inclined to save ourselves for the Stilton and a barley wine.

Recipes to try Carrot borscht (page 14); Baked beer & chicory soup with Maroilles croutons (page 16); Ham with Coke & stout (page 99); Steak & ale pie (page 93); Cottage pie with porter (page 96); Carbonnade of beef with Orval (page 91); Fabada (page 103); Japanese-style winter vegetable stew with miso (page 128); Welsh rabbit leeks (page 130); Baked apples with winter ale (page 149).

" Beer is all too often served too cold or too hot: lager and light beers, icy cold; ales, warm and unpleasantly soupy. Pilseners, lagers, blonde ales, wheat beers and fruit beers should be lightly chilled. More robust ales should be served at cellar temperature. "

A beer at all hours

The great thing about beer is that you can drink it at any time of day or night. Here, I recall my initiation into an authentic weisswurst breakfast, while Will fantasizes about his perfect beer day.

Weisswurst breakfast

The first thing to learn about the great Munich tradition of the weisswurst breakfast is that it must be consumed by noon. No self-respecting Münchener would eat it any later, except on special occasions. The sausages must also be made fresh, which means heading off early for the region's butchers.

In appearance and texture, weisswurst are not dissimilar to a boudin blanc – ivory pale and very smooth. Like other fresh German sausages, they must be made only from meat – in this instance, veal and pork – without any rusk, colouring or chemical additives, and the characteristic seasoning being pepper, nutmeg, lemon zest and parsley. They should be poached in hot, barely simmering, water for about 20 minutes, and they are never grilled.

There's an elaborate ritual to eating them. Traditionally, they are sucked from the skin through the hole at the end of the sausage, a technique that has its own name 'zuzeln', Bavarian slang for sucking, and is just as inelegant as it sounds. An acceptable alternative is to cut them lengthways and deftly peel off the skin with your knife. Either way they are utterly delicious – light, fresh and tangy with their perfectly matched accompaniments of mild sweet mustard, large soft salty pretzels and freshly drawn Franziskaner Weissbier. The 'never after noon' rule is occasionally overlooked on high days and holidays, such as Carnival and on Christmas Eve, when they are consumed after midnight mass. There's also a Bavarian custom at weddings that the groom's friends wake him with balloons at 4 in the morning and cook him a weisswurst breakfast. But, outside Munich, where you can buy them all day long, they're mainly consumed for 'frühschoppen' or a mid-morning snack. 'Normally, you wouldn't say "I'm having a beer" around 10 o'clock in the morning, but with a weisswurst you can,' I was told.

Will's beer day

0700 – Red Eye Wake up with a head like a sore bear and a mouth like Gandhi's flip flop. Time for a restorative Red Eye, a blend of beer and tomato (or 'clamato' juice), which can include raw egg. This drink is a beer-centric alternative to the Bloody Mary and can contain just as many variants. It's apparently very popular in Calgary, Canada. Wonder why…

0900 – Porridge and Oatmeal Stout This sounds pretty Scottish, although, in fact, the inspiration comes from the Gotlands Bryggeri micro-brewery on the Swedish island of Gotland. According to beer hunter Michael Jackson, they brew an Oat Malt Stout there and are into their porridge, which gave me the idea of linking the two. Not the lightest of breakfasts, perhaps, but one that should at least keep hunger at bay until elevenses.

1100 – Smoked beer, smoked salmon and bagels A smoked fish mid-morning snack sounds like nothing out of the ordinary in either Germany or Alaska, and both those countries do a damn fine line in smoked beers. Try Schlenkerla Rauchbier for an admittedly quirky but stimulating mid-morning pick-me-up.

1300 – Ploughman's lunch and a pint of bitter One of the best lunches known to man – achingly simple to do. All you need is bread (thickly and unevenly sliced, please), cheese (lots of it), pickles, a slice or two of really good ham and something green and crunchy (think apples, celery, spring onions…) and a pint of cool, hoppy bitter like Young's. The quintessential English pub lunch.

1430 – Postprandial snooze and an Alhambra Negra After all those carbs, you'll probably need to come over all Spanish and have a bit of an afternoon snooze. What better way to lull you into your siesta than a small glass of cool Spanish beer – a tried-and-tested formula throughout the Iberian peninsula? Personally, I favour Alhambra Negra (a dark lager from the Cervezas Alhambra brewery in Grenada).

1800 – Pint of SNPA (Sierra Nevada Pale Ale) and a few pretzels After such a hard day, you'll need picking up again, or need to go out for a drink with someone who genuinely has had a tough day at work. Seriously, I don't think there's anything more restorative than a SNPA and a pretzel or two. Strong, dense and very hoppy, SNPA is the perfect early evening drink.

2000 – Dinner Not that I strictly need it, but when has that ever stopped me? I'm not going to overdo it, though – just a glass of Deus (brewed in Belgium, aged for a month in barrels in Champagne), some moules frîtes with a Westmalle Tripel (yeah, I know Mum doesn't think that's the best match with mussels but tough…) and a few (well, alright, the best part of a box) of Belgian chocolates with Liefmans Kriek, a sour cherry-flavoured beer. Magic.

2330 – Just a quick one for the road Risk several hours of sleeplessness with a caffeine-rich nightcap of Meantime Coffee Beer, which uses Fairtrade coffee beans (see page 147). Finish the chocolates and drift off counting beers rather than sheep.

Will's beer-based drinks & cocktails

It might seem like sacrilege to combine beer with other ingredients but there are perfectly respectable precedents for doing so. Syrups and bitters have been added to beers for years to combat excess bitterness or acidity, while the tradition of mulling beer goes back several centuries, to at least Shakespeare's time. Obviously, you wouldn't use your very best craft beers, any more than you'd make a cocktail with a bottle of Krug or a mulled wine with Mouton-Rothschild.

Black Velvet

(*Illustrated left*) A basic supermarket champagne or sparkling wine is fine for this.

makes 6–8 glasses

2 x 330ml bottles of Mackeson or Guinness, well chilled
1 bottle of champagne or sparkling wine, well chilled

Carefully fill the glasses just under half full with the stout. Slowly top up with champagne or sparkling wine.

'Champagne' Cocktail

The perfect party drink for sniffy friends who think that beer is downmarket.

makes 20 glasses

1 bottle of apricot brandy
  (actually an apricot liqueur) *
5 x 50cl bottles of light lager, such as Peroni,
  well chilled
a bottle of Angostura bitters
You will need champagne glasses

Pour a splash (1–1$\frac{1}{2}$ tbsp) of apricot brandy and a couple of drops of Angostura bitters into the bottom of each glass. Top up slowly with lager, tilting the glass towards you as you pour. Stir with a swizzle stick or a spoon handle.

* The amount of apricot brandy you use depends on the lager you're pouring and your own personal taste.

Michelada

This is a popular way of drinking beer in Guadalajara, Mexico. We serve it like this at Green & Red, mixed with fresh lime juice and served long over ice.

makes 1 glass

25ml lime juice
4–6 dashes Maggi liquid seasoning or Worcestershire
  sauce
2–6 dashes hot chilli sauce
pinch of sea salt
a bottle of Dos Equis or other light lager

Put the first four ingredients into a highball glass full of ice cubes and stir. Top up with a nice cold beer, preferably Dos Equis, but it works with any light lager.

Dog's Nose

This is a great mulled beer recipe that we got from Gary Regan of Ardent Spirits (www.ardentspirits.com). It came with a hilarious introduction, which, sadly, we don't have room to print here, but you'll find it on Mum's website (www.matchingfoodandwine.com). You can also use a mixture of ale and porter, in which case add a little ginger to the recipe. The Dog's Nose then becomes a Pearl. Don't ask me why.

makes 1 glass

350ml Guinness, at room temperature
2 tsp brown sugar
50ml Beefeater or other full-strength gin
freshly grated nutmeg

Pour the Guinness into a sturdy glass and heat it on high in a microwave for about a minute. Add the brown sugar and gin, and stir gently. Sprinkle over a little grated nutmeg.

Hawksmoor
Shandy

Picon-bière

Mum's Midsummer Cup

(*Illustrated left*) A delicious ale-based version of Pimm's using Plymouth Fruit Cup. You may need to change the proportions, depending on which beer you use, so taste as you go.

serves 4–6

250ml Plymouth Fruit Cup, chilled

500ml fruity golden ale, such as Badger's
  Golden Glory, chilled

250ml traditional white lemonade, chilled

10–12 ice cubes

fresh apple, orange and cucumber, sliced

sprigs of mint for decoration

Pour the Plymouth Fruit Cup into a large jug. Add the ale and lemonade and stir. Add the ice cubes and slices of apple, orange and cucumber. Decorate with mint.

Hawksmoor Shandy

(*Illustrated on previous page*) A refreshing shandy with a twist from Nick Strangeway, the ever-inventive mixologist/manager at Hawksmoor (our steak restaurant and cocktail bar in London).

makes 1 glass

25ml Beefeater gin

12.5ml lemon juice

5ml sugar syrup

5 mint leaves + extra for garnish

a couple of shakes of Angostura bitters

Sierra Nevada Pale Ale

a slice of lemon, to garnish

Put the first five ingredients in a shaker full of ice. Shake, double strain and top up with Sierra Nevada Pale Ale. Garnish with lemon and mint.

Picon-bière

(*Illustrated on previous page*) A retro French drink, based on Amer Picon, a bitter aperitif developed in the early 19th century as an anti-malarial treatment for French soldiers fighting in Algeria.

makes 1 glass

150ml blonde beer, chilled

20–30ml Amer Picon

Pour the Amer Picon into a glass and top up with the beer.

Lamb's Wool

A slight adaptation of a traditional mulled ale recipe in *The National Trust Book of Christmas and Festive Day Recipes* by Sara Paston-Williams (Penguin, 1983). Perfect for Christmas Eve.

serves 8

8 small Cox's or other flavoursome eating apples

2 x 550ml bottles Newcastle Brown or other brown ale

1/2 bottle inexpensive sweet wine such as a Greek muscat

1 cinnamon stick

a blade of mace

6 cloves

a finely pared strip of unwaxed lemon peel

6–8 tbsp soft dark brown sugar

Preheat the oven to 200°C/400°F/Gas 6.

Score round the centre of each apple with a sharp knife. Put them in a lightly oiled baking dish and roast for 25–30 minutes until soft. Meanwhile, heat the brown ale, wine, spices, lemon peel and half the sugar in a large saucepan, taking care not to let the liquid boil.

When the apples are cooked, peel away the skin and add them to the ale and spices in the pan, breaking them down as much as possible. Cover and leave for half an hour for the flavours to infuse.

Remove the lemon peel and cinnamon, and strain the mixture through a sieve, squashing and pushing through as much of the apple as possible. Reheat the mixture gently, stirring, again taking care not to let it boil. Check for sweetness, adding extra sugar if needed. Serve in earthenware or heatproof glass mugs.

Food with beer

Here are some suggestions for what to eat with your favourite beers (see also A beer for all seasons, page 168).

British bitters & pale ales
Classic British pub food: sandwiches; ploughman's, cold meats and pork pies; fish and chips; hot cheese dishes, such as macaroni cheese and welsh rabbit; vegetarian bakes with root veg. With stronger ales: roasts; casseroles; steak pies; sausage and mash; anything with an onion gravy. Hoppier ales can handle a bit of spice.

IPAs
Will pair well with many dishes that go with British bitters (see above) but they're best with curries. American IPAs can handle stronger flavours, such as grilled salmon, barbecued and chargrilled meats, and mature farmhouse Cheddar. Also good with chicken liver pâté.

Light lagers, Pilseners & Kölsch
Simply grilled or fried fish; pickled herrings and other pickled and smoked fish, such as smoked salmon; sushi; pizza; light Mexican snacks, such as guacamole; kebabs; light seafood salads; borscht and other beetroot-based dishes.

Witbiers & weissbiers
Mildly spiced Asian-style salads and snacks; shellfish, especially crab and mussels (moules marinières); Thai and mildly spiced Indian curries; goats' cheese; asparagus; pasta and risottos with spring veg; omelettes; quiches.

Blonde ales & strong golden ales
Any food with a creamy sauce or dressing, especially chicken and salmon; other salmon dishes, such as salmon en croute and fishcakes; chicken Caesar salad; chicken pot pie; rich shellfish, like scallops and lobster; dishes based on sweet vegetables, such as corn, red and yellow peppers, and butternut squash.

Belgian tripel ales
Similar dishes to the above but also good with rich pâtés and very rich creamy cheeses and blue cheeses.

German- & Czech-style golden lagers
Roast, grilled or fried chicken; pork or veal escalopes; spaghetti carbonara; pretzels; sliced German sausage and potato salads; grilled bratwurst; choucroute.

Viennese-style lagers, amber ales & lagers
Beer and cheese soups; fondue; gutsy pasta dishes, like spaghetti bolognese and veggie or meat lasagne; moussaka; roast pork, chicken and turkey; Spanish-style dishes with chorizo, like fabada; Mexican meat dishes like lamb birria; sheep's cheeses.

Dark lagers
Strongly flavoured vegetable dishes such as those based on beetroot, mushrooms and aubergine; smoked sausages; pâté; grilled or pan-fried venison; dishes flavoured with miso; soba noodles.

Dark Trappist beers & bières de garde
Prime candidates with (and in) big beefy stews, like carbonnades; roasts, especially roast lamb with garlic and rosemary; French bistro dishes, like duck confit and cassoulet; steak and mushrooms; cheese, especially strong washed-rind cheeses, like Epoisses, and Swiss cheeses like Gruyère; a cheeseboard.

Sour red ales, such as Rodenbach Grand Cru
Duck and feathered game, like pheasant; roast lamb.

Gueuze
Pot roast pheasant and other game casseroles; oily fish, such as mackerel; rillettes; coarse-cut meaty terrines; choucroute and other dishes that include sausage and cabbage; salads; curry (a surprising but very successful recent discovery).

Brown ales
With lighter styles, like Manns: traditional British dishes, similar to those under British bitters and pale ales (see above). More robust American styles: burgers, especially with blue cheese; barbecues; Mexican and American Southwest dishes flavoured with smoked

chile, like chile Colorado; dishes flavoured with five spice or hoisin sauce; bean hotpots.

Stouts
Oysters and other shellfish-based dishes like creamy chowders and smoked fish pies; scallops; boiled gammon or bacon; stews or gravies made with stout; light chocolate desserts.

Porters & imperial stouts
Similar to the above but you can rachet up the flavour intensity. Smoky ham dishes; sticky barbecue sauces; dark, dark stews; anything with black pudding; rich chocolate desserts.

Smoked beers
Depends on how pronounced the smoke flavour is but in general smoked meats, especially ham; smoked fish, especially hot-smoked fish; barbecue and spicy rice dishes like jambalaya or joloffe rice; smoked cheese.

Barley wines & other sweet beers, such as tripel bocks
Stilton and other blue cheeses; dried fruits; rich fruit cakes; caramel and nut-based desserts, like treacle tart and pecan pie; vanilla, toffee or brown bread ice cream.

Fruit beers
With raspberry and cherry beers: chocolate desserts, especially with berries; creamy desserts, like pannacotta and cheesecake; tarts or other desserts with summer berries; salads that include berries; white-rinded cheeses like Brie and Camembert; duck. With peach, mango and passion fruit beers: creamy desserts or salads that include those fruits.

Honey beers
Light chicken, ham or cheese salads.

Ginger-flavoured beers
Oriental dishes, such as stir-fries; crab.

Chocolate beers
Tiramisu; coffee and banana-flavoured cakes and desserts.

Coffee beers
Dark chocolate tarts and cakes.

Beer with food

This isn't by any means a comprehensive list but a quick, easy-reference guide to the things we – and, we hope, you – like to eat. If you don't find what you're looking for, check out the index, the introductions to each chapter or my website (www.matchingfoodandwine.com).

Asparagus **Witbiers; light Pilseners**

Barbecues **Amber ales; brown ales; lightly smoked beers**

Beef **Traditional English ales; dark Belgian abbey or Trappist beers**

Cakes (fruit) **Barley wines**

Cheese (see pages 140–1)

Cheesecake **Cherry and raspberry beers**

Chicken (see also page 67) **Golden ales and lagers; Viennese-style lagers; summer ales (with chicken salads)**

Chilli con carne **American brown ales; Viennese-style lagers**

Chinese **Witbiers with dim sum and seafood; Belgian brown ales with duck and beef dishes**

Chocolate **Porters; cherry and raspberry beers**

Couscous **Golden ales and lagers**

Crab **Belgian-style witbiers**

Curries **IPA and hoppy pale ales**

Duck **Strong belgian ales; cherry- and raspberry-flavoured beers**

Fish and chips **British bitter**

Fish pie **Pale ales; stouts (with smoked fish)**

Gammon **Hot: stout; porter; smoked ales. Cold: golden ales or lagers. Smoked hams are also good with smoked beers**

Goose **Gueuze; bières de garde; sour red ales**

Ham See Gammon

Herrings (pickled) **Pilseners**

Ice cream **Doppelbocks**

Lamb **Strong British or Belgian ales; sour red ales**

Mexican **Viennese-style lagers**

Mushrooms **Dark lagers; brown ales**

Mussels **Witbiers; gueuze**

Noodles **Light wheat beers; Pilseners**

Oysters **Stout; Pilseners**

Pasta (see page 41)

Patés **Pale ales; fruit beers; tripel ales**

Pecan pie **Barley wines**

Pork **Viennese-style lagers; amber ales; saisons**

Prawns **Pilseners; witbiers; golden ales (depends on the seasoning)**

Pumpkin pie (see Pecan pie)

Risotto **Light Pilseners; wheat beers**

Salads (see also page 121) **Witbiers; weissbiers; fruit beers; summer ales**

Salmon **Strong golden ales and lagers**

Sausages **German style: golden lagers. English style: best bitters; pale ales**

Smoked fish **Pilseners**

Soups (see also page 13) **Lighter soups: pale ales. Mushroom and other stronger flavours: dark lagers**

Spaghetti bolognese **Amber ales; saisons**

Steak **Strong British or dark Trappist ales; saisons**

Stir-fries **Witbiers or similar wheat beers**

Sushi **Japanese lager**

Thai food **Witbiers or weissbiers**

Tiramisu **Chocolate or coffee beer**

Tuna **Canned: pale or golden ales. Seared: IPA**

Turkey (see also Chicken) **The bigger flavours can take a stronger beer like an amber ale; pumpkin-flavoured beers can also be good.**

Vegetarian dishes (see individual recipes)

Venison **Similar beers for Beef or try a malty Scottish ale**

Where to buy & drink good beer

Shops

We know that supermarkets aren't a bad place to pick up a beer these days but a) you already know about them, and b) the guys below need your custom if the independent sector is to survive.

The Ale Cellar 24 Woodland Terrace, Darlington, Co Durham DL3 9NU
www.alecellar.com

BarleyCorns 42 Welsh Row, Nantwich, Cheshire CW5 5EJ
www.barleycorns.co.uk

The Offie 142 Clarendon Park Road, Leicester LE2 3AE
www.the-offie.co.uk

Open All Hours 5 St. Johns Street, Keswick, Cumbria CA12 5AP
www.oahkeswick.co.uk

Open Bottles 131 Taunton Road, Bridgwater, Somerset TA6 6BD
no website

Tuckers Maltings Teign Road, Newton Abbot, Devon TQ12 4AA
www.tuckersonline.co.uk

Utobeer Borough Market, London SE1 1TL
www.utobeer.co.uk

Online

1516 Beer Company www.1516beer.co.uk
specializes in organic, gluten-free and vegetarian beers

Beers of Europe www.beersofeurope.co.uk

Beers of the World www.beerclubofbritain.co.uk
runs a beer enthusiast's scheme with a quarterly selection

Beer-pages www.beer-pages.com
Tom Cannavan and Roger Protz's beer site

CAMRA beer club www.camrabeerclub.co.uk

Cellarman www.cellarmandirect.com
real ales delivered in 5-litre mini casks

James Clay & Sons www.beersolutions.co.uk
one of Britain's biggest and best trade suppliers

Little Beer Shop www.littlebeershop.co.uk
specializes in real ales brewed in Norfolk and Essex

LivingBeer.com www.livingbeer.com
specializes in bottle-conditioned beers

Onlyfinebeer www.onlyfinebeer.co.uk
choice of over 1,300 beers and ciders

Pitfield Beer Shop www.pitfieldbeershop.co.uk
now only trading online and at farmers' markets

www.specialitybeermerchants.com
Belgian beer specialists, headed by Master Beer Sommelier Marc Stroobandt

www.realale.com
runs a real ale club

Pubs

Just a few, and an admittedly personal selection, of the many pubs that serve good food and great beer. For a far more comprehensive guide, buy Susan Nowak and Jill Adam's excellent *Good Pub Food* (CAMRA Books).

The Anchor Main Street, Walberswick, Suffolk 1P18 6QA
www.anchoratwalberswick.com
Mark Dorber's pub (formerly of The White Horse, Parsons Green, London)

The Anderson Union Street, Fortrose, Inverness IV10 8TD
www.theanderson.co.uk

The Angel Coaching Inn High Street, Heytesbury,
Wiltshire BA12 0ED
www.theangelheytesbury.co.uk
owned by TV chef Antony Worrall Thompson

The Drunken Duck Barngates, Ambleside, Cumbria
LA22 0NG
www.drunkenduckinn.co.uk
has its own brewery attached

Fence Gate Inn Wheatley Lane Road, Fence,
Lancashire BB12 9EE
www.fencegate.co.uk
run by a butcher who makes his own sausages

The Fox 28 Paul Street, London EC2A 4LB
www.thefoxpublichouse.co.uk
award-winning gastropub

The Horseshoe 28 Heath Street, London NW3 6TE
Australian-run brewpub

The Marquess Tavern 32 Canonbury Street, London
N1 2TB
www.marquesstavern.co.uk
Will's pub, so we had to include that, didn't we?

The Narrow 44 Narrow Street, London E14 8DP
www.gordonramsay.com
the first of Gordon Ramsay's new pub estate

The Pot Kiln Frilsham, nr Yattendon, Berks RG18 0XX
www.potkiln.co.uk
TV chef, Mike Robinson's pub

The Talbot at Knightwick Worcester WR6 5PH
www.the-talbot.co.uk
brewpub serving locally sourced and organic food

Thomas Rigbys 23–5 Dale Street, Merseyside L2 2EZ
0151 236 3269
50 different beers and beer matches on the menu

The White Horse Parsons Green, London SW6 4UL
www.whitehorsesw6.com
Iconic London pub

Restaurants & brasseries

Anthony's 19 Boar Lane, Leeds LS1 6EA
www.anthonysrestaurant.co.uk
molecular gastronomy and beer

Aubergine 11 Park Walk, London SW10 0AJ
www.auberginerestaurant.co.uk
the first UK Michelin-starred restaurant with a good beer list

Brew Wharf 1 Stoney Street, London SE1 9AD
(Borough Market)
www.brewwharf.com
busy Belgian-style brasserie and micro-brewery

Hawksmoor 157 Commercial Street, London E1 6BJ
www.thehawksmoor.com
Will's American steakhouse, specializing in American craft brews

The Lowlander branches in Drury Lane and the City,
London
www.lowlander.com
brasserie specializing in Belgian and Dutch beers

Le Manoir aux Quat' Saisons Church Road, Great
Milton, Oxford OX44 7PD
www.manoir.com
top chef Raymond Blanc has become a born-again beer lover

Market Restaurant 104 High Street, Manchester M4 1HQ
www.market-restaurant.com
serious speciality beer list

Quilon 41 Buckingham Gate, London SW1E 6AF
www.thequilonrestaurant.com
top-end Indian restaurant hosting regular beer events

Online beer & food resources

www.beercook.com
website of American beer writer Lucy Saunders

www.matchingfoodandwine.com
Fiona's website, which also includes beer and other drinks

www.specialitybeermerchants.com/beer-and-food
see Online, above

Conversion charts

Volumes (assumes all spoon measures are level)

1 tsp	5ml
2 tsp	10ml
1 tbsp	3tsp/15ml/1/2fl oz
2 tbsp	30ml/1fl oz
3 tbsp	45ml/11/2fl oz
4 tbsp	60ml/2fl oz
75ml	21/2fl oz
90ml	3fl oz
100ml	31/2fl oz
120ml	4fl oz
150ml	5fl oz
200ml	7fl oz
240ml	8fl oz
250ml	81/2fl oz
300ml	10fl oz
350ml	12fl oz
400ml	14fl oz
450ml	15fl oz
500ml	17fl oz
600ml	1 pint
750ml	11/4 pints
900ml	11/2 pints
1 litre	13/4 pints
1.2 litres	2 pints
1.5 litres	23/4 pints
1.7 litres	3 pints
2 litres	31/2 pints
3 litres	51/4 pints

Weights

grams	ounces
10g	1/4oz
15g	1/2oz
20g	3/4oz
25g	(scant 1oz)
30g	1oz
45g	11/2oz
50g	13/4oz
55g	2oz
75g	21/2oz
85g	3oz
100g	31/2oz
115g	4oz
125g	41/2oz
140g	5oz
150g	51/2oz
170g	6oz
200g	7oz
225g	8oz
250g	81/2oz
280g	10oz
300g	101/2oz
340g	12oz
400g	14oz
450g	1lb
500g	1lb 2oz
550g	11/4lb
600g	1lb 6oz
675g	11/2lb
750g	1lb 10oz
800g	13/4lb
900g	2lb
1kg	21/4lb
1.1kg	21/2lb
1.5kg	3lb 3oz
1.8kg	4lb
2kg	41/2lb

Acknowledgements

Many thanks to all those who have helped with this book, particularly Nigel Stevenson of James Clay for giving us a first-hand experience of cuisine a la bière over in Belgium, Joachim Oertel and his colleagues at the CMA for introducing us to the delights of the Oktoberfest, and the Craft Brewers Association for giving us access to the Great American Beer Festival. Thanks, too, to those who provided beers for recipe testing and tastings, especially Utobeer, Rupert Ponsonby and Natasha Claxton of R & R Teamwork, St Peter's Brewery, Badger Ales, Black Sheep and the Meantime Brewery.

Many, many thanks to CAMRA for letting us loose on this book, especially to Roger Protz for suggesting the idea, to Jo Copestick for being brave enough to commission us, and to Simon Hall and Debbie Williams for seeing it through. Special thanks to Vanessa Courtier, Angela Boggiano and Jules Mercer for making the food look so great and being such a joy to work with, and to Helen Ridge for her unerring eye for a typo.

Thanks to all at The Marquess Tavern for putting up with our endless photoshoots and, last but not least, to Trevor and Maria, our other halves for consuming endless beers and beer recipes (not that you should feel too sorry for them...).

Fiona Beckett

I'd like to thank the various people who helped and inspired me here – Utobeer (Borough Market) have been particularly helpful. Thanks, obviously, to my mother, who got me interested in eating and drinking too much in the first place. Also, to my wife Maria, who shares the passion with me, and to Huw, my business partner, who helps me make a living from it.

Will Beckett

Index

A

aioli, red pepper 55
almonds
  Bakewell tart 154–5
Alsace-style onion tart 33
antipasti 38–9
apples
  baked apples with winter ale 149
  choucroute 101
  Emmental, fennel & apple salad
    124–5
  Lamb's Wool 177
  pot roast pheasant with bacon, onion
    & apple 80
  potato & apple purée 84
apricot pancakes 152
artichoke, bacon & Taleggio pizza 34–5
aubergine parmigiana 131
avocados
  avocado salsa 117
  Green & Red's guacamole 23

B

bacon
  bacon, artichoke & Taleggio pizza
    34–5
  choucroute 101
  fabada 103
  pot roast pheasant with onion, apple
    & 80
  smoky bacon bolognese 43
Bakewell tart 154–5
balsamic vinegar
  beer & balsamic-glazed onions 139
banana tatin 146–7
barbecue sauce 72–3
barley wines 179
barm brack 151
batter
  fish & chips 64–5
  quick fruit fritters 153
Bavarian potato salad 127
BCC barbecue sauce 72–3
beans
  chile Colorado 116–17
  fabada 103
  mushroom moussaka 133
beef
  (almost) doner kebabs 30–1
  carbonnade of beef with Orval 91
  chile Colorado 116–17
  cottage pie with porter 96
  smoky bacon bolognese 43
  steak & ale pie 93
  steak with Innis & Gunn 86–7
  ultimate roast beef sandwich 28
beer
  comparing with wine 9

cooking with 11
  matching food & 8–10, 178–81
beer-can chicken 72
beetroot
  beetroot & cream cheese spread 23
  carrot borscht 14–15
  sweet & sour herring, beetroot &
    potato salad 59
bhajias, crispy onion 107
bières de garde 178
bistro blinis 58
bitters 178
black-eye beans
  mushroom moussaka 133
black pudding
  fabada 103
  roast pork belly with 84
Black Velvet 173
blinis, bistro 58
blonde ales 43, 178
blueberry & peach beer jellies 160
bolognese sauce 43
borscht, carrot 14–15
bread 134–5
  Gorgonzola & pear bruschetta 143
  Maroilles croûtons 16–17
  sandwiches 28–9
  spicy crab crostini 54
  sunflower seed & stout bread 136
breakfast, weisswurst 170–1
brown ales 101, 178–9
bruschetta, Gorgonzola & pear 143
butternut squash, chestnut & wild
  mushroom fusilli 44

C

cabbage
  chunky potato, onion & cabbage
    soup 19
  spiced juniper cabbage 80
cakes
  barm brack 151
  dark, sticky Christmas cake with
    prunes & Guinness 151
carbonation 8–9
carbonnade of beef with Orval 91
carrot borscht 14–15
champagne
  Black Velvet 173
  'Champagne' Cocktail 173
cheat's chicken korma 108
cheese
  Alsace-style onion tart 33
  aubergine parmigiana 131
  bacon, artichoke & Taleggio pizza 34–5
  beer & cheese fondue 142
  beetroot & cream cheese spread 23
  cheese, onion & potato pie 33

Emmental, fennel & apple salad
    124–5
  Gorgonzola & pear bruschetta 143
  Liptauer cheese spread 22
  Maroilles croûtons 16–17
  matching beer to 140–1
  Paul's cracking cheese straws 20
  roasted Red Leicester, red onion &
    sweet pickle sandwich 29
  salmon burgers with goats' cheese
    & sun-dried tomatoes 57
  Welsh rabbit leeks 130–1
cheesecake, summer berry 155
cherries
  chocolate & cherry roulade 156
  raspberry & cherry beer jellies 160
cherry beer sorbet 159
chestnuts
  roast butternut squash, chestnut &
    wild mushroom fusilli 44
chicken 66–77
  beer-can chicken 72
  cheat's chicken korma 108
  chicken Caesar salad 76
  joloffe rice 118
  light blonde gravy for chicken 69
  Oktoberfest chicken 68
  Sierra Nevada chicken 75
chicken liver pâté with cognac 27
chickpea, garlic & yoghurt dressing 30
chicory
  baked beer & chicory soup 16–17
chilli
  chile Colorado 116–17
  Green & Red's guacamole 23
chocolate & cherry roulade 156
chocolate beers 179
choucroute 101
Christmas cake with prunes &
  Guinness 151
chutney, mint & coriander 107
Coca-Cola, ham with stout & 99
cocktails 172–7
cod
  fish & chips 64–5
  smoked fish pie 60
coffee beers 147, 179
coriander & mint chutney 107
cottage pie with porter 96
crab
  crab, prawn & dill fishcakes 55
  spicy crab crostini 54
crayfish
  joloffe rice 118
crostini, spicy crab 54
croûtons, Maroilles 16–17
curries
  cheat's chicken korma 108

rogan josh 111
Thai green vegetable curry 113

D

desserts 144–9, 152–63
dips & spreads
  beetroot & cream cheese spread 23
  Green & Red's guacamole 23
  Liptauer cheese spread 22
Dog's Nose 173
dressings
  chickpea, garlic & yoghurt 30
  honey, mustard & yoghurt 124–5
  piquant 122
  raspberry beer 78
  soy & sesame 122
dried fruit
  barm brack 151
  dark, sticky Christmas cake 151
drinks 172–7
duck
  duck & Kwak 79
  smoked duck salad with raspberry
    beer dressing 78
  spicy duck noodles 112–13

E

Emmental, fennel & apple
  salad 124–5
entertaining 164–81

F

fabada 103
fennel
  Emmental, fennel & apple salad 124–5
  mussels with fennel & witbier 51
  prawn, fennel & leek risotto 47
fish, smoked & pickled 58–63
fish & chips 64–5
fishcakes, crab, prawn & dill 55
fondue, beer & cheese 142
food, matching beer & 8–10, 178–81
French-style chicken liver pâté 27
fritters, quick fruit 153
fruit beers 160, 179

G

gammon
  ham with Coke & stout 99
ginger-flavoured beers 179
golden ales 178
Gorgonzola & pear bruschetta 143
gravy 98
  light blonde gravy for chicken 69
guacamole, Green & Red's 23
gueuze 80, 178
Guinness
  Black Velvet 173

dark, sticky Christmas cake with
  prunes & 151
Dog's Nose 173
Guinness & oysters 50–1
ham with Coke & stout 99

H

haddock
  fish & chips 64–5
  smoked fish pie 60
ham
  ham & parsley pâté 27
  ham with Coke & stout 99
Hawksmoor Shandy 177
herring, beetroot & potato salad 59
honey beers 179
honey, mustard & yoghurt dressing
  124–5
honey-spiced nuts 20

I

Innis & Gunn, steak with 86–7
IPAs 111, 178

J

Japanese-style winter vegetable stew
  with miso 128
jellies
  blueberry & peach beer 160
  mango & passion fruit beer 160
  raspberry & cherry beer 160
joloffe rice 118

K

kebabs, (almost) doner 30–1
Kölsch 178
Kwak, duck & 79

L

lagers 178
lamb
  (almost) doner kebabs 30–1
  lamb birria 114
  rogan josh 111
  shearers' stew 90–1
Lamb's Wool 177
leeks
  prawn, fennel & leek risotto 47
  Welsh rabbit leeks 130–1
Liptauer cheese spread 22
liver
  French-style chicken liver pâté 27

M

mango & passion fruit beer jellies 160
mayonnaise
  red pepper aioli 55
meat 82–103

menus 167
Michelada 173
mint & coriander chutney 107
moussaka, mushroom 133
mulled beef 173
Mum's Midsummer Cup 177
mushrooms
  fat pork chops with Duvel &
    mushrooms 87
  mushroom & mustard soup 18
  mushroom moussaka 133
  roast butternut squash, chestnut &
    wild mushroom fusilli 44
  Sierra Nevada chicken 75
mussels with fennel & witbier 51

N

noodles, spicy duck 112–13
nuts, honey-spiced 20

O

Oktoberfest chicken 68
onions
  Alsace-style onion tart 33
  beer & balsamic-glazed onions 139
  cheese, onion & potato pie 33
  chunky potato, onion & cabbage
    soup 19
  crispy onion bhajias 107
  roast parsnip & onion soup 15
  rogan josh 111
Orval, carbonnade of beef with 91
oysters, Guinness & 50–1

P

pale ales 108, 178
pancakes, apricot 152
parsnip & onion soup 15
passion fruit
  mango & passion fruit beer jellies 160
pasta 37, 40–5
  roast butternut squash, chestnut &
    wild mushroom fusilli 44
  smoky bacon bolognese 43
pastrami on rye sandwich 29
pâtés
  French-style chicken liver pâté 27
  ham & parsley pâté 27
peaches
  blueberry & peach beer jellies 160
pears
  Gorgonzola & pear bruschetta 143
pecan nuts
  smoked duck salad 78
peppers
  joloffe rice 118
  red pepper aioli 55
pheasant with bacon, onion & apple 80

pickled fish 58–63
Picon-bière 177
pies
    cheese, onion & potato pie 33
    cottage pie with porter 96
    smoked fish pie 60
    steak & ale pie 93
Pilseners 178
piquant salad dressing 122
pizza 34–5
    bacon, artichoke & Taleggio 34–5
ploughman's lunch 138–9
pork
    fat pork chops with Duvel &
      mushrooms 87
    roast pork belly with black pudding 84
    sticky barbecued ribs 88–9
porter 179
    cottage pie with porter 96
potatoes
    Bavarian potato salad 127
    cheese, onion & potato pie 33
    chunky potato, onion & cabbage
      soup 19
    cottage pie with porter 96
    fish & chips 64–5
    potato & apple purée 84
    sausages & stoemp 100
    Sierra Nevada chicken 75
    smoked fish pie 60
    sweet & sour herring, beetroot &
      potato salad 59
prawns
    crab, prawn & dill fishcakes 55
    prawn, fennel & leek risotto 47
prunes, dark, sticky Christmas cake
    with Guinness & 151

R
raspberries
    Bakewell tart 154–5
    raspberry & cherry beer jellies 160
    summer berry cheesecake 155
raspberry beer dressing 78
red kidney beans
    chile Colorado 116–17
redcurrants
    summer berry cheesecake 155
rice 37
    joloffe rice 118
    prawn, fennel & leek risotto 47
rogan josh 111
roulade, chocolate & cherry 156

S
salads 120–1
    Bavarian potato salad 127
    chicken Caesar salad 76

Emmental, fennel & apple salad 124–5
    smoked duck salad with raspberry
      beer dressing 78
    sweet & sour herring, beetroot &
      potato salad 59
salmon burgers with goats' cheese &
    sun-dried tomatoes 57
salsa, avocado 117
sandwiches 28–9
    pastrami on rye 29
    roasted Red Leicester, red onion &
      sweet pickle 29
    ultimate roast beef 28
sauces
    BCC barbecue sauce 72–3
    gravy 98
    light blonde gravy for chicken 69
    for pasta 40–1
    tartare sauce 64–5
sauerkraut
    choucroute 101
sausages 126
    fabada 103
    sausages & stoemp 100
    weisswurst breakfast 170–1
seafood 48–65
seasons, choosing beer 168–9
Shandy, Hawksmoor 177
shearers' stew 90–1
Sierra Nevada chicken 75
smoked beers 89, 179
smoked duck salad with raspberry beer
    dressing 78
smoked fish 58–63
smoked fish pie 60
smoked mackerel
    bistro blinis 58
smoky bacon bolognese 43
sorbets
    cherry beer sorbet 159
    weissbier sorbet 159
soups 12–19
    baked beer & chicory soup 16–17
    carrot borscht 14–15
    chunky potato, onion & cabbage
      soup 19
    mushroom & mustard soup 18
    roast parsnip & onion soup 15
sour red ales 178
soy & sesame salad dressings 122
spicy food 104–19
steak & ale pie 93
steak with Innis & Gunn 86–7
stews
    carbonnade of beef with Orval 91
    fabada 103
    Japanese-style winter vegetable stew
      with miso 128

shearers' stew 90–1
sticky barbecued ribs 88–9
stout 179
summer berry cheesecake 155
sunflower seed & stout bread 136
sweet & sour herring, beetroot &
    potato salad 59
sweet beers 179

T
tartare sauce 64–5
tarts
    Alsace-style onion tart 33
    Bakewell tart 154–5
    banana tatin 146–7
teabreads 150
    barm brack 151
temperatures, serving 169
Thai green vegetable curry 113
Thai tuna burgers with lime &
    coriander 57
tomatoes
    aubergine parmigiana 131
    avocado salsa 117
    fabada 103
    lamb birria 114
    mushroom moussaka 133
    salmon burgers with goats' cheese
      & sun-dried tomatoes 57
    smoky bacon bolognese 43
    sticky barbecued ribs 88–9
Trappist beers 91, 178
tripel ales 178
tuna burgers with lime & coriander 57
turnips
    sausages & stoemp 100

V
vegetables 120–1
    Japanese-style winter vegetable stew
      with miso 128
    Thai green vegetable curry 113

W
weissbier 178
    weissbier sorbet 159
weisswurst breakfast 170–1
Welsh rabbit leeks 130–1
wine, comparing beer with 9
witbier 178
    crab & witbier 54
    mussels with fennel & witbier 51

Y
yoghurt
    honey, mustard & yoghurt dressing
      124–5
    mint & coriander chutney 107

Books for beer lovers

CAMRA Books, the publishing arm of the Campaign for Real Ale, is the leading publisher of books on beer and pubs. Key titles include:

Good Beer Guide 2008
Editor: ROGER PROTZ

This 35th anniversary edition of the Good Beer Guide is the only guide you will need to find the right pint, in the right place, every time. It's the original and the best independent guide to around 4,500 pubs throughout the UK; in 2002 it was named as one of the Guardian's books of the year, and the Sun rated the 2004 edition in the top 20 books of all time! This annual publication is a comprehensive and informative guide to the best real ale pubs in the UK, researched and written exclusively by CAMRA members and fully updated every year.

Good Beer Guide Prague & The Czech Republic
EVAN RAIL

This fully updated and expanded version of a collectible classic is the first new edition to be produced by CAMRA for 10 years! It is the definitive guide for visitors to the Czech Republic and compulsory reading for fans of great beer, featuring more than 100 Czech breweries, 400 different beers and over 100 great places to try them. It includes listings of brewery-hotels and regional attractions for planning complete vacations outside of the capital, sections on historical background, how to get there and what to expect, as well as detailed descriptions of the 12 most common Czech beer styles
£12.99   ISBN 13: 978 1 85249 233 5.

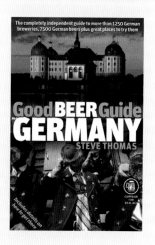

Good Beer Guide Germany
STEVE THOMAS

The first ever comprehensive region-by-region guide to Germany's brewers, beer and outlets. Includes more than 1,200 breweries, 1,000 brewery taps and bars and more than 7,200 different beers. Complete with useful travel information on how to get there, informative essays on German beer and brewing plus beer festival listings.
£16.99   ISBN: 978 1 85248 219 9

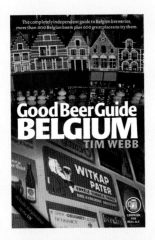

Good Beer Guide Belgium
TIM WEBB

Now in its 5th edition and in full colour, this book has developed a cult following among committed beer lovers and beer tourists. It is the definitive, totally independent guide to understanding and finding the best Belgian beer and an essential companion for any beer drinker visiting Belgium or seeking out Belgian beer in Britain. Includes details of the 120 breweries and over 800 beers in regular production, as well as 500 of the best hand-picked cafes in Belgium.
£12.99   ISBN: 978 1 85249 210 6

Beer, Bed & Breakfast
JILL ADAM & SUSAN NOWAK

A unique and comprehensive guide to more than 500 of the UK's real ale pubs that also offer great accommodation, from tiny inns with a couple of rooms upstairs to luxury gastro-pubs with country-house style bedrooms. All entries include contact information, details about accommodation, beers served, meal types and times, and an easy-to-understand price guide to help plan your budget. This year, why not stay somewhere with a comfortable bed, a decent breakfast and a well-kept pint of beer, providing a home from home, wherever you are in the country?
£14.99 ISBN: 978 1 85249 230 4

Good Pub Food
SUSAN NOWAK & JILL ADAM

This fully revised sixth edition of Good Pub Food singles out over 600 real ale pubs in England, Wales, Scotland and Northern Ireland, which also specialize in fine cuisine. All pubs are highlighted on easy-to-use maps and there are full descriptions of their locations, ales, menus, prices, vegetarian selections and facilities. Both Susan Nowak and Jill Adam have been involved in editing and compiling CAMRA guides for over 20 years.
£14.99   ISBN 13: 978 1 85249 214 4

Order these and other CAMRA books online at www.camra.org.uk/books, ask at your local bookstore, or contact: CAMRA, 230 Hatfield Road, St Albans, Hertfordshire AL1 4LW. Telephone 01727 867201

It takes all sorts to Campaign for Real Ale

CAMRA, the Campaign for Real Ale, is an independent not-for-profit, volunteer-led consumer group. We actively campaign for full pints and more flexible licensing hours, as well as protecting the 'local' pub and lobbying government to champion pub-goers' rights.

CAMRA has more than 86,000 members from all ages and backgrounds, brought together by a common belief in the issues that **CAMRA** deals with and their love of good-quality British beer. For just £20 a year, that's less than a pint a month, you can join CAMRA and enjoy the following benefits:

* A monthly colour newspaper informing you about beer and pub news and detailing events and beer festivals around the country.

* Free or reduced entry to over 140 national, regional and local beer festivals.

* Money off many of our publications including the Good Beer Guide and the Good Bottled Beer Guide.

* Access to a members-only section of our national website, www.camra.org.uk, which gives up-to-the-minute news stories and includes a special offer section with regular features saving money on beer and trips away.

* The opportunity to campaign to save pubs under threat of closure, for pubs to be open when people want to drink and a reduction in beer duty that will help Britain's brewing industry survive.

* Log onto www.camra.org.uk for CAMRA membership information.

Do you feel passionately about your pint? Then why not join CAMRA?

Just fill in the application form (or a photocopy of it) and the Direct Debit form on the next page to receive three months' membership FREE!

If you wish to join but do not want to pay by Direct Debit, fill in the application form below and send a cheque, payable to CAMRA, to: CAMRA, 230 Hatfield Road, St Albans, Hertfordshire AL1 4LW. Please note that non-Direct Debit payments will incur a £2 surcharge. Figures are given below.

Current rate		Direct Debit	Non-DD
O	Single Membership (UK & EU)	£20	£22
O	Concessionary Membership (under 26 or 60 and over)	£11	£13
O	Joint Membership	£25	£27
O	Concessionary Joint Membership	£14	£16

Life membership information is available on request.

Title _____ Surname _____

Forename(s) _____

Address _____

_____

Postcode _____ Date of Birth _____

Email address _____

Signature _____

Partner's details if required

Title _____ Surname _____

Forename(s) _____

Date of Birth _____

Email address _____

Please tick here O if you would like to receive occasional emails from CAMRA (at no point will your details be released to a third party).

Find out more about CAMRA at www.camra.org.uk

Instruction to your Bank or Building Society to pay by Direct Debit

DIRECT Debit

CAMPAIGN FOR REAL ALE

Please fill in the form and send to: Campaign for Real Ale Ltd. 230 Hatfield Road, St. Albans, Herts. AL1 4LW

Name and full postal address of your Bank or Building Society

To The Manager   Bank or Building Society

Address

Postcode

Name (s) of Account Holder (s)

Bank or Building Society account number

Branch Sort Code

Reference Number

Banks and Building Societies may not accept Direct Debit Instructions for some types of account

Originator's Identification Number

9	2	6	1	2	9

FOR CAMRA OFFICIAL USE ONLY
This is not part of the instruction to your **Bank or Building Society**

Membership Number

Name

Postcode

Instruction to your Bank or Building Society

Please pay CAMRA Direct Debits from the account detailed on this Instruction subject to the safeguards assured by the Direct Debit Guarantee. I understand that this instruction may remain with CAMRA and, if so, will be passed electronically to my Bank/Building Society

Signature(s)

Date

✂ detached and retained this section

This Guarantee should be detached and retained by the payer.

DIRECT Debit

The Direct Debit Guarantee

- This Guarantee is offered by all Banks and Building Societies that take part in the Direct Debit Scheme. The efficiency and security of the Scheme is monitored and protected by your own Bank or Building Society.

- If the amounts to be paid or the payment dates change CAMRA will notify you 7 working days in advance of your account being debited or as otherwise agreed.

- If an error is made by CAMRA or your Bank or Building Society, you are guaranteed a full and immediate refund from your branch of the amount paid.

- You can cancel a Direct Debit at any time by writing to your Bank or Building Society. Please also send a copy of your letter to us.